All too often, bickering couples turn molehills into mountains. In *Mom vs. Dad*, Tom & Lucy Riles prove that the view is better, and usually funnier, from the molehill. I think this book deserves a hashtag: #BickerBest

—Tom Bergeron, TV host and veteran husband

A true to life, humorous peek of his side/her side that will bring smiles and laughter to your heart. It confirms what I've always said, men are strange and women are weird…You'll love it.

—Dr. Kevin Leman, *New York Times* bestselling author
of *Sheet Music* and *Have a New Kid by Friday*

Tommy and Lucy just get it. I've always said, parenting is the hardest job on the planet, and marriage is the next toughest. These two have the ability to make you laugh and feel validated at the same time. *Mom vs. Dad* is an amazing book that proves parenting is a contact sport.

—Meredith Masony, founder of That's Inappropriate
and Filter Free Parenting

In *Mom vs. Dad*, Lucy and Tom Riles bring an entertaining and conversational approach to exploring the everyday challenges we face as partners and as parents. There's plenty of heart and humor in the real-life situations they explore, from sharing meals to sharing a phone charger. The result is a book that's eminently relatable, always thought-provoking, and reads like a fun conversation with friends.

—Carrie and John Pacini, co-founders, Mom 2.0 & Dad 2.0

What a fun and refreshing read this was for my wife and I! Lucy and Tom bring a relatable sensibility, hilariously covering topics which ALL OF US bicker about.

"Hey babe, don't touch the laundry that I LAY ON TOP OF THE HAMPER. I'm not sure whether it's dirty or clean, so please just leave it alone!"

Sorry about that. I'm back. So yeah, you should totally go buy *Mom vs. Dad*; it's like comedy and family therapy all in one!

—Taylor Calmus, creator of *Dude Dad* and host of *Super Dad* on the Magnolia Network

Watching Lucy and Tom take the gloves off and bicker with one another from a place of love and respect is not only endearing, but HILARIOUS. Every fight or disagreement in this book is something that my wife and I have locked horns on more than once! Use it for a good laugh with your partner, topics of discussion over dinner with other couples, or maybe even a way to address that ONE thing your spouse does that absolutely drives you nuts…*Mom vs. Dad* opens the door to achieving marital bliss…maybe.

—Adrian Kulp, author of bestselling *We're Pregnant! The First-Time Dad's Pregnancy Handbook* and founder of award-nominated parenting blog *Dad or Alive*

Tommy and Lucy Riles *for sure* have a camera set up in our house! We laughed hysterically at the relatability of each topic. If you're looking to enjoy a good read with your spouse that includes a little lighthearted banter, it's *Mom vs. Dad*.

—Chris and Lindsay Balmert, Team Balmert

Finally, Tommy and Lucy Riles have come up with the definitive rule book concerning parenting. This unintentional sequel to the groundbreaking book *The Joy of Sex* could easily have been called *The Misery of Kids*. In this comprehensive and hilarious contest for the title of "head of the household," they lay out the terms for the ultimate battle of *Mom vs. Dad*. And although I'm still pretty sure I'm going to lose most, if not every argument with my wife, at least now I know why. This should be required reading for any couple who are thinking about having kids.

—Jamie Kaler, actor, comic, and creator of The DadLands

Mom
vs.
DAD

Mom vs. DAD

The Not-So-Serious Guide to the Stuff We're All Fighting About

LUCY & TOM RILES

WORTHY®

New York • Nashville

Worthy
Hachette Book Group
1290 Avenue of the Americas, New York, NY 10104
Worthy.com
twitter.com/Worthy

First Edition: November 2020

Worthy is a division of Hachette Book Group, Inc.
The Worthy name and logo are trademarks of Hachette Book Group, Inc.

The publisher is not responsible for websites (or their content) that are not owned by the publisher.

The Hachette Speakers Bureau provides a wide range of authors for speaking events. To find out more, go to www.hachettespeakersbureau.com or call (866) 376-6591.

Unless otherwise noted, photos are courtesy of the authors.

Library of Congress Cataloging-in-Publication Data
Names: Riles, Lucy, author. | Riles, Tom, author.
Title: Mom vs. Dad : the not-so-serious guide to the stuff we're all fighting about / Lucy Riles and Tom Riles. Description: First edition. | Nashville : Worthy, 2020.
Identifiers: LCCN 2020022706 | ISBN 9781546036890 (hardcover) | ISBN 9781546036876 (ebook)
Subjects: LCSH: Parenting—Miscellanea. | Parents—Attitudes. Classification: LCC HQ755.8 .R5319 2020 | DDC 306.874—dc23
LC record available at https://lccn.loc.gov/2020022706

ISBN: 978-1-5460-3689-0 (hardcover), 978-1-5460-3687-6 (ebook), 978-1-5491-5764-6 (downloadable audio)

Printed in the United States of America

LSC-C

1 2020

To our children, Barbara, Tommy, Scotland, and Katie,
thank you for being YOU! We love you more.
We love you most. We love you to the moon and back.
We love you to infinity and beyond. No comebacks.

To our fur babies, Duke and Duchess, thank you
for loving all of us on the good days, the bad days,
and every day in between.

To our precious angels, our son Scotland and Lucy's mom,
Barbara, your souls are a daily reminder for us to
do better, love deeper, and always appreciate
the gift of life. You will forever live in our hearts
until we meet again.

Contents

Introduction

Hello and welcome to *Mom vs. Dad: Whose Side Are You On?*
   I'm Tommy.

And I'm Lucy.

And we've been married since 2008.

We actually met playing in a coed softball league in LA. I was a veteran player and one of the original members of the league when this rookie strolled on in wearing his orange New York Mets visor. I played catcher, which allowed me to get in the heads of the batters. You see, I may not have had the physical strength to hit a home run, but I had a way to charm the cleats off players. And since the league had a ten-to-one guy-to-girl ratio, the odds were in my favor. I was also from the South Side of Chicago so I was especially good at small talk. Unbeknownst to me, one particular player took notice…at the time, I only took notice of his repeated infield pop-ups.

Lucy was the only player to wear a cowboy hat and jean shorts. She was hard to miss. When I stepped up to the plate the first time and saw her, a different mission became my objective. My future wife was playing catcher as I batted, and suddenly the game of baseball didn't matter. I wanted a different type of home run. (Damn, I'm smooth!)

It was six months before I even knew who this Mets fan was. But once I did, and after just a few weeks of dating, I knew I had found my future husband and my future children's father. Within eleven months, we were engaged, and we married eighteen months after that.

It was around that time that we realized we had very different takes on just about everything. Naturally, we both thought our way of living was the "right" way.

Welcome to marriage.

Then we started having kids. And, well, they just made things more complicated. There was more stress in our home and more stuff to disagree about.

Welcome to parenthood.

We didn't always see eye to eye; we still don't. But we love each other. And we made a vow to stay together forever. And gosh darn it, that's what we're going to do.

Here's the thing, when it comes to the small stuff, Tommy and I could not disagree more. But when it comes to the big stuff, the truly hard and heartbreaking stuff, our love is unbreakable.

To give you an idea of what I'm talking about, I lost my best friend, my mom, nine months after we got married. She was diagnosed with stage 4 metastatic melanoma and was given less than a year to live. Tommy and I had anything but a blissful newlywed stage that first year of marriage. Tommy's vows were immediately tested as he cared for his new wife who was going through one the hardest times of her life.

We love your mama, and always will!

Then came a devastating diagnosis twenty weeks into my pregnancy with our first child. Our baby had very serious heart defects and was given a 1 in 2,500 chance of surviving the pregnancy and making it to birth. Doctors explained the best-case scenario was that she would make it to birth…We were devastated. But at thirty-nine weeks and five days, our miracle baby girl arrived. Three days after that, she went through open-heart surgery to save her life. Hours after that, she flatlined three times in front of us, nurses and doctors reviving her each time. Today, our thriving baby is ten years old! And just like her namesake (my mom), Barbara loves puppies, art, and creative writing!

Believe in miracles, y'all. I tuck mine into bed every night!

Barbara is the strongest kid you will ever meet!

Over the past decade, we've been pregnant five times.
First, our miracle baby girl, Barbara.
Then came a hormonal miscarriage.

Then our healthy baby boy, Tommy.

Then a devastating stillborn loss of our precious angel, Scotland.

Last, our healthy rainbow baby of hope, Katie.

It's always tough for me to answer the question "How many kids do you have?" Physically, you will see only three in a Christmas card or Instagram post, but I know in my heart that I am a mom of four children. It's just not always the right scenario to share about my baby angel, Scotland. Surely the cashier at the grocery store is merely striking up small talk to be polite, not knowing what he is asking is a bit of a loaded question. Plus, I never want someone to feel bad or uncomfortable just for being kind and conversational. But it was important that I share my Scotland with you. So when you're flipping through this book and see family photos with only three children, yet my bio says I am a mom of four, you now know why. I am proud and honored to be a mom to all four of my children.

Okay, enough with the heavy stuff; this book is meant to be fun and light, to help you and your partner acknowledge and laugh together over the things that make you different. I promise. I simply bring it up because Tommy and I are going to poke a lot of fun at each other, and the gloves will come off. But I want you to know this all stems from a profound place of love and respect. The fact that we've gotten to a place in our marriage where we can laugh and tease each other about petty, quirky habits is an absolute blessing…we know this and we don't take it for granted. We've known loss, despair, and heartbreak. But we are living, breathing examples that there can be JOY after loss and HOPE after despair and you will genuinely be able to LAUGH again after heartbreak…all things I didn't think were possible five short years ago.

So when I tease Tommy about his twenty-year-old cargo shorts, just know it's all relative.

We may disagree on everything (even though I'm clearly right most of the time), but that doesn't actually matter in the grand scheme of things.

When we started covering all of the topics we're about to discuss in this book in our stage show and on our podcast, we were surprisingly overwhelmed with how relatable it seemed to be to other couples and parents. When the little things start to feel like big things in the heat of the moment, know that they're not. It's not a deal breaker. Agree to disagree, find the laughter and levity in it, and then get on with loving each other.

In a nutshell, this book will let you see that you are not alone. Let these topics we discuss reassure you that other couples bicker over the same petty little things too. Every day, all day.

Now that we got all that out of the way, buckle up, Tommy, because you are about to get roasted!

I love you too...even more than all of my boxes of childhood keepsakes. (I'm not a hoarder at all.) I'll never let you or them go.

About This Book

First and foremost, the GOLDEN RULE for this book is as follows:

This book is meant to be fun…not an excuse to start bickering with your spouse. Instead, we hope one of these topics speaks to you so much that you find yourself nudging each other and saying, "That's so you!" followed up with "No, that's you!" followed by realizing, "Wow, we are not the only ones who feel this way!" We know living with someone is hard. But what if there were a playful way to approach these little battles you face with your partner rather than fodder for an all-out war? Well, that is exactly what this book is all about.

We hope *Mom vs. Dad: Whose Side Are You On?* engages you to interact with us and each topic we battle about. It should be an interactive experience for you and your partner to enjoy. We are going to leave the decision completely up to a third party to vote on…YOU! As you read through the various topics, you get to vote for the position you like to think is right.

Some ground rules on how to get the most out of your experience:

1. Don't take yourself too seriously. So you hate that your husband leaves the toilet seat up. Have a little fun with him and cover it with saran wrap. If your wife refuses to make the bed, short sheet her. Then laugh as your partner tries to figure out what the heck just happened.
2. Most couples, yes, even your picture-perfect neighbors, bicker over the same things. Feel validated in knowing you are not the only one who secretly dreams of making a big bonfire with your partner's "vintage" cargo shorts.

3. Include your partner. Read aloud or bring it out on your next date night in after the sitter canceled last minute or your little one got sick. If you read only one topic that leads to laughter and a fun conversation with your spouse, our job is done.

4. Don't go in aligning yourself with one party. Just because you are a dad doesn't mean you will always align with Tommy or the dad's side...you might actually be surprised how much you both flip-flop sides.

5. More than anything, we hope this book is "nudge-worthy" to you. We want you nudging your partner as you read; we want you two sharing a laugh; we want this book to act as a reason to connect.

6. This is not meant to replace marriage therapy. This is more a lighthearted exploration of the little idiosyncrasies that make you annoyed, not that make you want to divorce. If there are deeper issues that need to be addressed (we've certainly been there), seek professional help. Now, if you are trying to prove your partner wrong about the proper way to install a toilet paper roll, seek us!

7. And if you find that this book is completely unrelatable because you don't bicker with your partner, congratulations on being the only couple on planet Earth that doesn't bicker...you either live in separate homes or haven't been married long enough.

Listen, when you have been married for years with multiple kids and dogs, and a fish named TJR, you are bound to run into a few disputes with your partner…okay, maybe more like a thousand. Maybe you find the exact things that attracted you to marry this person are now some of the same things that drive you absolutely crazy. And guess what? That's completely normal! At least it is for us, and based on thousands of couples who have attended our live show and listened to our podcast, it is for them too!

Now go have some fun!

Lucy and Tommy

Mom
vs.
DAD

Should My Wife Wear Heels on Vacation? And If So, Does She Have the Right to Complain About Her Feet Hurting?

I love taking trips with my wife. Just the two of us on a little getaway. Being out of town for a couple of days helps our relationship tremendously. Lucy and I would both agree that these mini trips have really helped our marriage in so many ways. (And massive shout-out to my parents, who usually watch the kids to make these getaways possible.)

However, Lucy and I have very different visions of what we do once we start our vacation. I like to walk and explore a city. I can walk around for multiple hours every day, and I make it a goal to see everything. Lucy has her own approach. The sights and attractions of a city aren't on her priority list. What is at the top of her vacation priority list is where we will eat dinner and what she will plan to wear for that dinner. Getting dressed up is a central feature of Lucy Vacation Planning. (And she looks good! Damn...)

Since she loves fancying up, she often comes down with HEELITIS. Let me explain.

On vacation, my wife likes to wear high heels. I'm talking the crazy stiletto spikes. The platform espadrille and then some wedges. The, yes, very sexy but also very torturous strappy sandals with a railroad spike for the heel. Those kinds of high heels. And having been with her for thirteen plus years now, I know this means she'll be complaining about her feet hurting within five minutes of us heading out on the town, and then we have to take cabs all around the city. I can't pay all those dollar bills for cabs, y'all.

HEELITIS is the Riles clinical name for the foot pain that results from donning and walking in footwear that was designed for wearing only if one is sitting or if one is standing in one spot all night long. From my extensive research on the subject (i.e., watching Lucy all these years) I've learned that high heels were never designed to actually be walked in. HEELITIS is a very predictable condition, always occurring when one's wife insists on wearing heels in a walking situation. So, Lucy's insistence on walking around on these torture stilts means that I am required to do some serious planning ahead.

While visiting Las Vegas, we had dinner reservations at the casino next door. She wanted to take a cab. Yes, you heard me, she wanted to take a cab to the casino next door. It would have been much harder because the cab would have had to drive around multiple hotels just to get next door. Granted, "next door" can mean quite a few steps in Las Vegas, so earlier in the day, knowing that my wife would be going to dinner in heels, I walked multiple routes to the hotel next door to find out the quickest way. I felt like I was in the Secret Service, checking the route to make sure it was safe for the president.

With a route that started in the lobby, taking an escalator to the parking garage, and crossing a service road, we made it to the casino next door in the least number of steps possible. HEELITIS AVERTED. Mission accomplished.

On a recent New York City trip, we were excited to be going to dinner and a Broadway show. I totally understood why my pretty bride wanted to get dressed up. However, we were planning multiple stops all over town throughout the evening, including some sightseeing that would require a bit of walking.

The subway in NYC is great. My first job out of college was in NYC, so I know the transportation system well, and in this situation, I thought it was best to get a subway card for the day. My wife started out walking to the subway station in heels, but I very quickly predicted her future foot pain. While she stopped at Starbucks, I ran back to the room and grabbed some flip-flops. She carried her heels in a bag until we arrived at the restaurant and show, and boom, it worked out great. HEELITIS AVERTED. And listen, I don't claim to be a fashion expert, but the female residents of New York City go by this method all the time, wearing sneakers with their power suits and cocktail dresses, dangling their designer sling-backs from their pinkies in a devil-may-care manner. If it's good enough for those fashionistas, why not my girl?

But my biggest question is, since my wife looks so good regardless, isn't it okay if she brings along some proper sneakers so we could do some walking around town?

Picture this.

There is this mom. She's been a stay-at-home mom (SAHM) for a decade now. Her day-to-day life plays out in a house where dishes, laundry, homework, and constant mess are never ending. Showering doesn't happen nearly as often as she would like. Most days, the only time she leaves her house is for her kids' school pickup and drop-off, and for dance or baseball practice. The only adult she sees regularly is her husband, and the rest of the time she is surrounded by mini dictators who fight, whine, place demands and negotiations on her until she's at their mercy. Because she is literally on the run all.the.time, she's in "proper sneakers" morning, noon, and night. And when her kids are finally asleep, she only has enough energy left to kick off those proper sneakers, eat Pringles, and drink wine while watching crappy reality shows on Bravo.

That mom is me.

But every once in a while, about two to three times a year, something truly glorious happens. Something that allows me to take off my suburban mom persona and replace her with Vacation Lucy. And let me tell you something…everyone loves Vacation Lucy, especially my husband, Tommy!! These two, maybe three times a year my husband and I leave the kids with family (very loving and capable family, lest you be concerned) and we get the heck out of Dodge! Vegas is driving distance for us so that always seems to be a staple spot we go to annually.

Now "Vacation Lucy"…

- showers daily;
- naps daily;
- drinks cold cocktails poolside daily; and,
- at night, dresses up in fun, sexy outfits that include high heels.

And if you've been to Las Vegas, you know one single hotel can be up to a mile radius, not to mention the half mile you have to walk from your hotel room to the elevators. So, when Vacation Lucy comes to Vegas, Vacation Lucy does not want to walk the Strip at night. My husband enjoys doing marathon walking courses around the Strip. But do you know what else my husband enjoys?! The hot, sexy outfits and heels I wear.

And you ladies know that the higher the heel, the thinner the leg looks…and Mama needs all the help she can get for slimming down those thighs, if you know what I'm saying!

He tells me, "Just wear flats," or, "Bring an extra pair of shoes," which don't exactly fit in the clutch I've packed to go with my dress. Plus, I'm officially in my forties now. Vacation Lucy has to compete with twenty- and thirty-years-olds with tight tushes and breasts that haven't fallen or encountered milk-sucking leeches that bless you with stretch marks. Mama may be past the age of wearing skintight pleather but she can still rock a LBD (little black dress)…if my heels are high enough!

Moral of the story, women want to look and feel their best. Especially SAHMs like me who don't get out much. We want a reason to get our hair and nails done, to throw on that dress and heels we love but never wear. So yes, when I finally have an occasion to dress up and spend quality time with my husband, order the short cab ride…it's a forgettable expense for a chance at an unforgettable night (wink wink).

And, for the record, it's totally false about my feet hurting after five minutes. They hurt after about fifty minutes.

Well, they may not hurt until minute fifty, but you're already talking about it at minute five.

Alright, ladies and gentlemen, it's time for you to choose whose side you are on!

From the mom corner…Vacations are the time to bust out those sexy heels you've been waiting to take the price tag off of. They are the gateway accessory to accessing your vacation self. Everyone wins, including that husband of yours.

From the dad corner…A vacation wife looks good in whatever she is wearing! Sometimes, on vacation, it's okay to put on comfortable shoes for doing a little more exploring without worrying about foot pain. Then slip on heels when it's time for a fancy restaurant…

Whose side are you on…MOM or DAD?

Should You Share Food with Your Partner?

Growing up as the youngest of twelve kids meant a lot of things: I would never have control of the remote control, I would never get to sit shotgun, and I would always, always, always have to share everything! I had to share my clothes, which were hand-me-downs, never new. Not only did I have to share a bedroom, I had to share a bed with my two older sisters for most of my childhood as well. And when it came to food, the only option I had was to share. No individual Happy Meals for us: My parents bought in bulk and it was survival of the fittest. When my mom would pull up in the driveway, she would honk the horn, which indicated you were to come out front and help carry in the groceries. We kids would rush to the front porch, devouring whatever contents occupied those grocery bags. The snacks were always the first consumed, usually within minutes. And like hibernating bears, we consumed as much as our bodies would allow in order to last us until the next grocery run. If you did not do this, it was a diet of sticks of butter and generic canned tomato soup for the remainder of the week.

This sounds like you were competing in a reality show while growing up!

Now that I am a mom, I still have to share a lot of things that come with the mom territory. I rarely have control of the car radio and remote control, mostly because I just want my kids to stop fighting. I still share a bed with two other people; this time my husband and our littlest kiddo, who crawls into bed every night with us. And just about anything that enters my house is fair game for all to use.

First off, as I'm writing this, our littlest is indeed sleeping next to me, and it is 5:00 a.m. Yep, I'm sharing! That's a nice story that you told above about your history of sharing, and I can totally relate to buying in bulk; my parents did too. We likewise didn't do individual Happy Meals; it was getting the thirty-five-cent cheeseburgers on Tuesdays, which McDonald's offered. The family would be out the door for under three dollars. To this day, I do bulk food shopping at Costco, and then our little family SHARES the groceries.

When I ask you to share, all I want is two french fries from your takeout order. I just want to make sure they are safe for you to eat. Or if we're eating out, I'll ask for one bite from your entree. I don't want more than that. I just need a tiny taste, and then I'll go back to my meal. We share finances, a home, and everything in between. We should be sharing food. It's just what families do!

My tolerance for sharing food has expired. Especially when it comes to sharing food with my husband.

Right. But can I just get a *couple* of fries? I'm not asking for much over here. I'm your life partner, after all.

My past has made me quite indulgent and stingy with my food. I purchase excessive amounts of groceries to avoid having to share.

That's why you buy excessive amounts? I never knew there was a reason, I thought you were just consistently overestimating what our family's stomachs could consume in a given amount of time. Since there is so much food in the fridge after you excessively grocery shop, I eat like I'm in a race to help finish it all. It feels like another type of reality competition series.

One indulgence I most enjoy in life is going out to eat at a nice restaurant without the kids. I relish the endless options to choose from on a menu, the cook in the back waiting to make it just for me, where I can eat it warm and not have to do the dishes afterward. It's a glorious thing.

My husband, however, likes to order something different from a menu and then tries to share my meal.

I enjoy taking you out to restaurants! You always look beautiful. And yes, I want to order a couple of meals that complement each other so we can share. I've got my eyes on the warm pasta dish, and you get the steak. Or I'll get the flatbread pizza, and you order the giant salad. That's what a relationship is about, complementing each other. Helping to make each other better. Let's make our meal better by sharing.

Heck no! If you want what I have, order it yourself. Even with fast food, you won't order fries for yourself......and then you ask me for some of mine.

Exactly. I don't want *an order* of fries. I'm so glad we're finally on the same page here. All I want is *two* fries so I can taste that salty goodness. That's it. Please?

Order your own dang fries! (He really is insufferable about trying to share food.)

Actually, I'm insufferable about not wanting to waste food. As I was told growing up, we are so lucky to even have food on the table at all. Sharing food is the way it should be, and I'll never stop asking. If we ordered another order of fries for me, and I ate only two, that would be wasteful.

When we're out to eat, to demonstrate his take on the good old "treat others the way you want to be treated" angle, my husband will offer me a few bites from his entree.

Yes, here I am enjoying the most delicious chicken piccata of my life. The chicken is baked perfectly, the peas are on point. The lemon taste, the unbelievable capers. I am loving every second of this, and yes, I want the one I love the most to try this. (Then, simply in the name of symbiosis, shouldn't I get some of yours?) I'm just doing unto others as I would want done unto me. From a culinary standpoint.

"No thanks, dollface. I'm good with what I ordered." That's what he tells me. But then he will go with the lurking shark move where he sits quietly staring at my plate. And when I'm clearly not finished, he'll go in for the attack. He'll ask, "Are you going to eat all of that?" I am literally midbite and now I'm that much more motivated to eat all of it because of his comment.

So you're finishing your dish out of spite, rather than sharing with me? At a restaurant, Lucy often comes down with a condition known as "toss happy." She'll allow her plate to be removed from the table before it is empty. If she told the server, "We're still working on this," those are some of the most beautiful words I would have ever heard.

If I don't keep my eye on her, she'll place her napkin on top of her food, and the server will take it away, even though I still wanted to try a bite. I'm certain she would at times rather have it thrown away than allow me to have a few bites. I have to watch her like a hawk and offer assistance in eating whenever I can.

My favorite move at a restaurant would be the opposite of "toss happy." I like to wipe the plate completely clean. I'll take the bread and wipe up every last drop of my entree. The ultimate respect I can give the chef is returning the plate so clean it looks like it was never touched. Not many things embarrass Lucy more than this. I'm not only a member, I'm the founder of the "clean plate club."

I'm sure that I could come off spiteful and stingy. But when you are raised the youngest of a dozen kids, you learn early on the value of basic human necessities to survive. And, y'all, this mama's a survivor!

That's cool and all, but can I just have a couple of fries?

Alright, ladies and gentlemen, it's time for you to choose whose side you are on!

From the mom corner…As parents and partners, we may be required to share everything else in life, but draw the line with food. Your plate is YOURS and you deserve to eat what is on it in peace.

From the dad corner…As a married couple, you do share everything. Time, space, money, children, and everything in between. For that reason, without a doubt, we should be sharing food. At least a couple of bites, please!

Whose side are you on…MOM or DAD?

Should You Compliment a Spray Tan?

Let me start by saying I believe my wife is just as beautiful without a spray tan as she is with one. She's a stunning lady, it's as simple as that. But over the past few years, my wife has more frequently started to dye her skin orange. If we're going to an event, or she's heading out on a weekend away with her girlfriends, she might get a spray tan a day or two before.

When she comes home from a spray tan, it's very noticeable. It's noticeable because I then have an orange wife. After a couple of days as an orange wife, Lucy turns tan, and she is then ready for her event as a faux sun-kissed babe.

There are a few items of interest about your wife going orange for a couple of days. She immediately smells a little different, which is interesting. And then there is the showering thing. She tells me that she can't shower, because otherwise, this fresh new tan will streak. And forget about making out with her. Should that encounter get a little, say, sweaty, I'd then also be responsible for destroying the tan illusion since the color would not have had time to "set." So basically, this tan is a built-in chaperone to marital relations. The minute Lucy walks in the door as a fresh shade of orange, I'm regretting her getting the tan.

It's not that I speak with an uninformed negative opinion of going orange. I myself had a similar experience of "orange regret" heading into college back in '97. I had just graduated from high school and turned eighteen years old that same summer. Now, I grew up to be a pretty good kid. Never breaking my parents' rules or trying to act out, I wasn't one to go buy cigarettes, even when I was legal. My attempt at a rebellious decision that infamous summer was when I used Sun-In lightener for my brown hair. Who remembers Sun-In? Basically, you would spray this peroxide mixture on your hair and go hang out in the sun for a while. It was supposed to give your hair this sun-kissed look, those bad-boy blond tips that were all the rage in the mid-1990s. But let's recall that I have dark brown hair. Dark. And so this Sun-In experiment? This resulted in an orange mane when I started college. That's right, my opening act with a whole new population of potential friends and colleagues was with me sporting pumpkin hair. My fellow college freshmen started calling me Christopher Robin from Winnie the Pooh, because of my, well, orange hair. How about that for a first impression?

Let's just say I NEVER got any compliments for my orange hair, which is why maybe I don't throw out spray tan compliments like they are nothing.

Anyhow, when my wife comes home with a spray tan, I notice that she is now orange. I acknowledge it. Then I recently learned that she wishes I would compliment her spray tan. Huh?

It never dawned on me to compliment something that is fake.

Do you compliment fake teeth? If a man had hair implants, do you compliment that? It feels kind of awkward to me.

Oh, really, Tommy Riles? You shouldn't compliment something fake? Then I guess we should go back to real Christmas trees instead of the fake trees you force upon our family. You go on and on and on about how much more superior fake Christmas trees are than real ones…but they are FAKE. I don't know, to have you arguing for real in light of your Christmas tree philosophy, it feels kind of awkward to *me*. (See chapter 24, "Christmas Trees: Real vs. Fake.")

Wait, I'm not looking for compliments on a fake tree! I'm just happy that it is doing the job, and it was the right decision for us on so many levels.

Back to spray tans. I thought the correct protocol if you suspect somebody got a spray tan is that you just notice it, and move on.

Now that I know my wife would like a compliment for her spray tans, I'm going to go ahead and do it. But who's with me? Does this just seem like an odd thing to compliment?

Listen, folks, I haven't had a lot of reasons to leave my house over the past decade. Kids' school pickup, drop-off, doctors' appointments, the grocery store…I know, I know, I lead a VERY exciting life. Not. So, when I actually have something that takes me out of the house, inspires me to shower and put on a bra, Mama's gonna BRING IT.

The nails get manicured, the eyebrows get threaded, the hair gets trimmed, and the skin gets sprayed to match the likes of a bronze goddess. When I was growing up in Chicago, us midwesterners savored sunshine and baked our skin with baby oil and tanning beds. Nowadays the spray tan is a fantastic alternative. Mama wants to glow like JLo! So, the day before the big event or trip, I go to this fabulous fellow mama, Emily, who runs her whole spray tan magic business out of her guest bedroom while her kids are at school. She makes this pasty white, Scotch Irish American girl shimmer and shine into the bronze goddess she was born to be!

Moral of the story: If you suspect your wife made some sort of effort to look good, just compliment her. Whether it's a new outfit, hairstyle, makeup, or yes, even an orange spray tan that will eventually turn your lady into a beautiful bronze trophy wife…send a little love her way. She needs to hear it more than you'll ever know.

PS Let the record show that I will happily forgo any complimenting of my fake tan IF our family can start getting real Christmas trees again.

Complimenting spray tans it is! What I've learned is that I want to help lift my wife up at all times. I guess on this topic you've won me over, and I'm going to start complimenting. I want you to feel good. And if I ever use Sun-In again (maybe for our twentieth anniversary?) I'm going to expect a compliment from you.

With some of these topics, you've gotta learn what Baby Mama needs, accept it, and do it for her.

Alright, ladies and gentlemen, it's time for you to choose whose side you are on!

From the mom corner...If you see your spouse making an effort, throw a compliment their way!

From the dad corner...Complimenting spray tans, toupees, dentures, hair extensions, and a waxed eyebrow seems a little odd. But maybe this is one of those we have to call a draw and say that if your partner indicates that they need a compliment for something in the above category, just roll with it.

Whose side are you on...MOM or DAD?

Is It Okay to Correct Your Partner's Grammar and Spelling?

The person with whom I have chosen to betroth* likes to point out my spelling and grammatical* errors. Like he is somehow superior to me because he can spell. Last time I checked, I didn't marry my English teacher. I also did not seek out a soul mate who possessed a fondness for correcting other people's spelling…but somehow, I ended up marrying one of "those" types.

I am in no way superior to my stunning and thoughtful wife. She is much more empathetic, generous, supportive, and beautiful than me. But there is one thing at which I am much better than her: SPELLING.

Also, objection to your point above. The people need to know that you often ask me how to spell certain words and that asking on your part happens much more than the number of times I, unsolicited, correct you. Will you please admit that?

Never!

Now there are few things I despise more in this world than a person who gives unsolicited spelling and grammar corrections.

Let me step in here for a moment. Congrats! You spelled "unsolicited" correctly!

Cool, you know the English language really well. Good for you. Please continue to love it and write exquisite* sentences that raise your inner literate. No, for real, I'm not being sarcastic. If one of your talents includes being a phenomenal* speller, I applaud you.

You weren't being sarcastic, but you were being facetious. (Note: Lucy loves using the word "facetious," but I'll put money on the fact that she had no idea how to spell it until reading it here, right now. But that's okay, because like I said, she is MUCH better than me in many different areas.)

It's true; I did not know how to spell "facetious" until right now... That doesn't even look right. Are you sure it's spelled like that?

But what I am trying to get at is the second you project your grammar superiority* upon me, whether it be in the form of a social media comment, text message, or email, you go from being an English scholar to a jackass. (Pardon my French...spelling.)

I've never claimed to be an English scholar. A math scholar? Perhaps. I scored 710 in math on my SATs. I scored much lower on my verbal, so I took an SAT prep course. Then I scored even lower.

Yeah, I'm not even going to share SAT scores...that I took twice! I feel like that is incriminating information that can be used against me. Was I a bed wetter far too long? Absolutely! Will I share my SAT score? NO WAY!

Now, the only time it is okay to correct grammar is when someone specifically asks for help. I will sometimes ask my husband how to spell things. And I know he just loves it, breezily giving me the accurate spelling, the letters casually rolling off his tongue, quietly reveling in the fact that I am struggling to spell a word he mastered on a sixth-grade spelling test. Now, in this case, it's okay to correct my spelling because I am asking for help. If I didn't, just hush your mouth.

Think of it like parenting advice. People despise people who offer unsolicited parenting advice. Same goes for spelling and grammar.

I would argue that if somebody is blatantly wrong, it is my duty to share the correct spelling. I'm saving you from making the same mistake twice. A great football coach lets his star quarterback hear it if he makes a mistake. Even if you're Tom Brady, and you already know you messed up, it's your coach's job to help guide you toward success. Wait, bad example. I know I'm not your spelling coach. Unless you want one?

OMG, YOU ARE NOT MY COACH! Leave me and my grammatical* shortcomings alone!

Thank you for finally admitting your shortcomings. That's the first step in your spelling recovery program.

If I write something and butcher the spelling of it and you take it upon yourself to correct me, a fortysomething grown-ass woman, then you suck. I'm sorry. You just do.

You did it to yourself. You spelled wrong. Ma'am, it's actually your spelling that sucks. Not me.

A little backstory on my literary saga that will hopefully garner some sympathetic support.

When I was in elementary school, my mom enrolled me in the Reading Clinic in downtown Chicago. It was easier for me to memorize the order of the sight words than to actually read them. Safe to say spelling, grammar, and reading were never my strengths. Don't get me wrong; I had many talents, like lip-synching the heck out of "Leader of the Pack" off my basement jukebox* and memorizing all the lines from Shakespeare's *Measure for Measure*, in which I played the leading role, Isabella. But when it came time to be called on to read the next paragraph aloud in school, I sounded like Forrest Gump, only with a thick Chicago accent. When I was in the eighth grade, some of the boys in my class came up with an oh-so-kind and endearing nickname for me…"Miss Illiterate."

Meanwhile, these knuckleheads were in the same special reading group as me. Hypocrites*!

Aw, babe, that's a sweet story. I didn't know that.

Cut to thirty years later, and I am now a seasoned woman in her forties. I've lived a little…I've lost a little…and I've loved a lot. Life has crushed me, bent me, tried to break me, but has also given me the most beautiful and blessed experiences. Each year is an absolute privilege* that I do not take for granted. I've learned what matters in life, and correcting other people's spelling and grammar is NOT one of them!

My dad wasn't the best speller, either, but he is one of the greatest humans I've ever encountered. And he has a saying: "I'm a lover, not a speller."

Now, I don't claim to be one of those great humans, but I have a saying too. It goes:

> "I may not be the sharpest crayon in the box, but I'm colorful nonetheless."

*All the words spellchecker corrected for me.

Alright, ladies and gentlemen, it's time for you to choose whose side you are on!

From the mom corner...Only correct your partner's spelling or grammar if they ask! Can I get an amen?

From the dad corner...Better spelling and grammar makes the world a better place. I'm just here to make the world a better place. Correct your partner's spelling as often as you can!

Whose side are you on...MOM or DAD?

Phone Charger Etiquette: Should You Unplug Your Partner's Phone to Charge Your Own?

I'm going to really try to come from a place of love, but, y'all…my husband's phone charger etiquette is for the birds!

I like the phrase "phone charger etiquette." I'm here to listen. I've got a few minutes because my phone is currently charging. It was down to 5 percent, and after a search around the house, I found your charger!

Ladies and gentleman, he's got jokes! But this is no joking matter. We probably have seven or eight perfectly functional phone chargers in our home. But when it comes time to charge our phones, we are lucky if we can find one. So, I created a simple solution, a phone charger home base. For our house, it's an outlet in the kitchen that acts as the hub for phone chargers. This home base was thoughtfully chosen because it is a high-traffic area and close to the hub where Tommy and I keep our keys and sunglasses. That way, when you leave the house or return from being away, you've got the basket for the keys, a shelf for the sunglasses, and a charger for the cell phones.

And if we always keep at least two chargers there, *both* our phones are sure not to run out of battery power. Perfectly logical solution, right?

But instead of spending any time and effort looking for his own dang charger, he will take the one remaining charger from my thoughtfully placed home base and move it to another place in the house…and then forget where he put it.

Wait, until I read this, we've never had a discussion about that being "the hub." I usually have to search everywhere to find where you have left a charger.

To quote Buddy the Elf, "You sit on a throne of lies!"

That…or you have selective hearing, which I hear is a common condition among spouses.

You see, I live with a swindler who cheats the phone charger etiquette system and takes advantage of me, a rule-abiding phone charger citizen. Since my husband's ability to find a phone charger that he misplaced is zero for eight, he strolls right up to my charger and does the unthinkable. He proceeds to unplug MY phone to charge his own! His excuse is something to the effect of "I'm going into work and my phone is at 52 percent and since you are home all day, you can charge yours later." Meanwhile, my phone lies unplugged at 11 percent.

Is that unthinkable, or is that just family sharing? (Read more about our different takes on sharing in chapter 2, "Should You Share Food with Your Partner?")

"BUT IT IS MY CHARGER! FIND YOUR OWN BLEEPING CHARGER!!" I curse in my head without actually bleeping.

They are OUR chargers. "When we married, we became one. I promised to love you for better or worse, in times of low phone battery or fully charged. I promise to share phone chargers till death do us part." That's what's going on in my head.

And his completely calm, unaffected tone makes me even more incensed. But that's not even the worst part…there is another thing my dearly beloved husband does that sets me over the edge of domestic sanity.

The following is an actual transcription of an ongoing conversation we have weekly, if not daily:

Me: Babe, where is the phone charger?

Him: I don't know.

Me: Where did you last charge your phone?

Him: Maybe check [insert several areas of home where there is no said charger].

Me: Not there.

Him: Where did you last leave it?

Me: *(Thinking, "Oh no, he is not going to turn this on me.")*
Found it.

Him: Where was it?

Me: In your work bag.

(Silence.)

Do you know how many outlets are in our house? A lot. And do you know how much time it takes me to check outlet after outlet? A long time. Of course, given the above record, I admittedly should probably just start with his work bag and make my way to the outlets from there.

I will battle you to the end about most topics in this book, but this right here, I will admit. I have a phone charger problem. Yesterday, I lost a charger and was looking from outlet to outlet. I moved the charger initially and forgot where I put it, so I had to search for another. You were out of town, so I couldn't blame you. It was then that I realized that I do indeed have a problem.

A few times too many each week, I find myself searching the house for those lifesavers. What would we be without power in our phones? I'm thrilled whenever I find a charger, and then I plug the phone into the outlet nearest to where I'll be spending the next few minutes. If I'm in the kitchen, I'll plug it there. If I'm in our bedroom, I'll plug it there. I'm guilty of plugging in for convenience rather than thinking of returning it to the charger home base (which we still haven't discussed as an actual thing, except for theoretically in this writing).

Selective hearing.

I'm going to admit something else right now too. (You're welcome for my admitting I'm wrong.) I'm totally guilty of leaving way too many phone chargers in my backpack. I'll bring a charger to and from work, and then forget that it was sitting in my bag when I arrive home.

Sometimes two to three chargers can be found in my backpack. Like I said, I have a charger problem.

Now that I've confessed, I'd like for you to admit that you take chargers from this supposed "home base" hub every day. You put them in your purse or in the outlet nearest the bed, and they are often rotating between those locations, until they are lost. I have so graciously apologized above; now it's your opportunity to admit some fault, with the world as our witness.

I will admit that I am a stubborn, fiery Scotch Irish old broad who has a hard time apologizing and admitting wrongdoing…but I stand firm in my actions when it comes to this matter. The only reason I take chargers from the home base and put them in my purse is because I am a mom who needs to be available at any time because I have kids. So when my phone battery is dying and I have to leave the house, and there is only one of eight chargers accountable, I bring it with me. Now IF the home base system were put into effect by both responsible parties, we would have two chargers permanently at the main hub and six more available for other uses.

I'm happy to join you at any time on the search for the missing phone chargers that you (okay, mostly I) have lost. It can be our shared mission. Because I love you.

I love you too. However, I do not love your phone charger etiquette and will not share in this fault that is yours and only yours.

What's worse, my husband's charger usage and locating issues don't even factor in what will happen once our kids have phones and chargers. Judging by the number of items my kids lose while also putting 0 percent effort into searching and 100 percent expectation on me doing the finding, along with the genetic predispositions from their father…

I'm basically screwed.

And you love us. So you forgive us. Thank you, we accept your forgiveness.

Alright, ladies and gentlemen, it's time for you to choose whose side you are on!

From the mom corner…Even in a committed, respectful, sharing marriage, phone chargers should not be seen as shared property. They were not specifically mentioned in the marriage vows, ergo, they remain separate from the "better or worse" clause.

From the dad corner…He admits when he's wrong, and he knows he has some weaknesses in this argument. But he will continue to unplug his wife's phone to charge his own every now and then. Especially if they are fighting and he wants to get under her skin…

Whose side are you on…MOM or DAD?

Is Amazon the Greatest Parenting Blessing or a Family Budget Curse?

Motherhood is the most important and rewarding job I will ever do in my life. But motherhood is also hard, y'all. It can be defeating and overwhelming and you will worry more than you ever knew was humanly possible. It comes with the territory...so is it worth it? ABSOLUTELY!

With that said, I'm going to dabble in some of the challenges that come with raising young children. At the top of most moms' lists of "least desirable things to do with your kids" would be getting them ready to leave the house. First, they have to find their shoes because Lord knows they are not in the designated shoe bins that Mom has conveniently placed by both front and back doors. About fifteen minutes before I plan to leave anywhere with my kids, I ask them to get their shoes on, knowing full well this will take a while, not in the actual donning of the shoes but in the locating of said shoes.

Then come socks and jackets and usually a wardrobe change because they are either still in their pajamas or not dressed for the current climate. If it's ninety degrees out, my kids turn up wearing sweatpants and a sweatshirt. When it's forty degrees out, they are in tank tops.

Um, that sounds a bit like you, my love. Sweatshirt in the summer so you crank the air-conditioning. Blasting the heat in the winter so you can wear shorts. (See chapter 15, "Who Should Control the Thermostat?" for a full disclosure.)

Once that fight about what the kids are wearing is settled, they realize they now have to pee. Or when they were babies, they always always ALWAYS had poop blowouts in their diapers as soon as we put them into their car seats. Seriously. Every time.

And listen, I live in Southern California, so the lowest temps are usually in the forties, which is cold, but OMG, what the heck do moms do when it's fifteen degrees and snowing or pouring rain?!? I've considered moving to a different part of the country…but legitimately decided to wait a few more years until my kids can dress themselves! I swear, I'd rather my family be nudists for three months than suit them up in boots, hats, gloves, and snowsuits for a diaper run to the store.

You know who are the real heroes living among us? Moms who raise kids in arctic climates.

Another highly undesirable task is taking your kids to run errands after finally getting them ready to leave the house. Running errands with young kids never ends well. For example, if I take them to the bank because I need to get some cash, my kid loses her marbles because they are all out of orange-flavored lollipops. You know what I got when I went with my dad to the bank? Nothing! Next, I have to go to the post office, which is incapable of having anything but excruciatingly long lines. While waiting, my kid successfully angers the woman behind the counter because he keeps swinging on the ropes, which I calmly told him a dozen times not to do, because I don't want to be judged as the yeller mom. Last up, I need to run to the store for Pull-Ups because one of the kids still wets the bed. (No judgment here, I was a bed wetter longer than I'd like to admit.) So you go to Target, but you have to first get past the three-dollar section that is strategically placed by the entrance. Thanks, Target. Kids are magnetically drawn to this slippery slope of seemingly cheap joy, and any hope for sanity is lost forever. Now everyone is crying because I won't buy them each a toy…on a Tuesday…in May…for no reason at all. You know what I got when I went to the store with my mom? Nothing!

That's exactly what they get when they go to the store with Dad nowadays…nothing!

By the time we get home, I've now developed a nervous tic while I wait for a suitable time to pour myself a glass of wine. Then I quote Oprah in my head: "Give it up to God, Lucy, give it up to God." It's something I say to myself. A lot. That and the Serenity Prayer.

Enter Amazon Prime. The savior to SAHMs like me. The mecca of access and convenience. And when you're a mom, convenience is king! Gone are the days of lugging that fifty-pound car seat carrier to the store to pick up diapers, wipes, bottles, pacifiers, poop bags, baby food, butt cream…they just show up at my front door. This was especially helpful when my babies were still literal babies, before they started school. No need to brush my hair or put on a bra. All thanks to Amazon, I could focus on cuddling and bonding with my babes.

I mean, one might even argue that Amazon has allotted me more quality time with my kids. Yes, Amazon has made me a better mother.

Okay, this topic hurts. In the wallet.

Amazon is awesome but it is TOO convenient. Next-day delivery? Same-day delivery? What? Before you have decided whether you actually need an item, it has already arrived.

And the sight of those Amazon vans coming down the street is just plain terrifying.

It used to be exciting to see a UPS truck. You see the deliveryman wearing shorts in the summer, with a big smile on his face. You get to know him.

But these Amazon vans and delivery folks...they're not there to get to know you. They drop a package, ring the doorbell, and run. It feels more like you're getting robbed, rather than receiving a gift.

The speed of the footsteps toward the door, the sound of the package hitting the ground, the doorbell ringing, and their engine restarting happens in a matter of seconds. And these villains will drop off three to four boxes at once.

With old-school UPS, every package your family received was a memory. The family opening the box together. Oh! A new croquet set from our cousins in Massachusetts. It's gonna be a happy summer after all.

With the speed of Amazon delivery, it feels more like your bank account is being drained than you are receiving something that you need. Our family recently took a long car drive to Texas (from California), and we drove throughout the night. The number of massive Amazon trucks you see on the road at 3:00 a.m. is astounding.

And the pain of an Amazon delivery sometimes begins even earlier. I'll see my wife on her phone in the middle of the night, and then I might get a glance at her emails the next morning and see "Your delivery is on the way..."

Ouch, ouch, and ouch.

And now you can order on Amazon by just talking to Alexa. "Alexa, we need some toilet paper." "Okay, we're on our way!" Footsteps. Package drop. Doorbell ring. Vroom, they're gone.

I've heard horror stories of kids ordering things on Amazon (via Alexa) without their parents even knowing. There are few things that would make my blood boil up more than knowing that my kids just ordered a gift of their own on Amazon, and the first I knew of it was when it showed up at our front door.

Wait, what happened? And where did all of our money go?

Alright, ladies and gentlemen, it's time for you to choose whose side you are on!

From the mom corner…Amazon quick delivery is the cornerstone of an evolved human society, and it is the saving grace of the mothering game. Don't fight progress, and don't make yourself crazy justifying every little Amazon purchase.

From the dad corner…The convenience of Amazon is great, but it has also become way too convenient to spend money. Amazon trucks, emails, and packages are stressful, and Amazon could be slowly turning our family's financials into our biggest enemy.

Whose side are you on…MOM or DAD?

Should Mom Compare All of Dad's Injuries to Childbirth?

My wife has delivered multiple beautiful babies for our family. She's a rock star, she's beautiful, she's amazing...

However, in the ten years since our first kid arrived, my wife has given me zero sympathy for any injuries I have encountered since. I mean, I've fallen off roller skates and broken a wrist, I've suffered serious bee stings that have enlarged and inflamed my ear, and a stubbed toe that once turned out to be a broken toe. Can I get a little love over here?

Let's break down these minor incidents...

Tommy was roller-skating for a skit on Life of Dad while I was home nursing a tongue-tied baby and chasing after a toddler. If you don't know this, tongue-tied babies have a very shallow latch, which makes breastfeeding excruciatingly painful. I endured this level of pain for five months until we clipped his tongue. Then there's my husband, making a choice to act over-the-top for the sake of the shot...even though he has not actually roller-skated in twenty years. He comes home wanting me to feel sorry for him for poor choices?

Where's the sympathy for all the pain I went through to nourish his namesake and the fact that my boobs will NEVER be the same because of it!?!

I mean, I think this is exactly my point. I feel terrible about the pain you were going through there, but does that mean I never deserve any sympathy?

Let's talk about that bee sting. Tommy and I were both walking our babies; I was pushing the toddler in a stroller, Tommy pushing our newborn in one of those bassinets on wheels that have no straps or buckles. I passed what looked to be a swarm of bees by a tree, with Tommy walking behind me. That's when I heard a shriek. Tommy had been stung by a bee. He immediately grabbed his ears with both hands...releasing our bassinet stroller, which headed toward the curb!!! We were on one of those streets where the sidewalk was directly next to the street. "Tom, THE BABY!" I yelled out, which quickly called attention back to the fact that he let go of our newborn, who was now headed toward grave danger! It could have been a whole lot worse than a friggin' bee sting, that's all I could think. Now listen, I know bee stings can hurt, but the timing and scenario legit garnered him zero sympathy from me. After all, I still had stitches from birthing his coveted child who will carry on his family name.

Lemme jump back in here for a second. First off, as I recall, I did let go of the stroller, but as it was rolling slowly into a shrub. I knew it was headed toward the bushes, and as expected, the stroller slowly glided to a stop in the bushes. Lucy was then the one who shrieked, overreacting to the stroller rolling toward the bushes, as I started damage control on my wounds.

My job, for fifteen plus years, has been entertaining audiences before a TV taping. I've worked for Ellen for years. (Yes, *that* Ellen. Yes, she is that awesome!) I showed up to work after the bee sting with a giant, red, enlarged ear. All of my coworkers and the audience members were like, "Hey, Tom, what's going on with your ear?" and, "Dude, is your ear okay?" and, "Are you really going to go talk to the audience with a giant, red, enlarged ear?" Well yes, I did. And no, it doesn't compare to "stitches from childbirth," but that's exactly my point! Don't compare, just throw me a little sympathy here!

And the broken toe…Tommy, why don't you tell everyone what happened right before you stubbed your toe in our dark bedroom. Now, unbeknownst to me, Tommy had just spent an hour doing dishes and cleaning the kitchen before bed. After he gets into the bedroom, I remind him that he didn't need to do all of that because our cleaning lady was coming the next day. Totally annoyed, Tommy uttered a very colorful phrase in my general direction, punctuating his upset about the situation. I kid you not, two milliseconds later, he trips over a piece of luggage and ends up breaking his toe. In other, totally unrelated news, Tommy's never used that expletive with me since!!

It was a joking expletive, and we both know that, lest you think I'm the mean cursing kind of guy. But the doctor sure wasn't joking when he said it was a broken toe and he put me on bed rest for three months.

Okay, I'm joking about the bed rest, but I did have a broken toe! And I kept walking the kids to school every day.

I get it, these two incidents don't compare to childbirth. And I would never dare compare them to childbirth. Remember, I have been a witness to the childbirth process, and watching it was painful enough. However, do I deserve zero sympathy when I am in pain? My kids feel bad for me, my dogs feel bad for me, the audience at *The Ellen Show* feels bad for me, but my wife does not?!?!

Now before Tommy goes off and paints me as a coldhearted ice queen, I am actually an immensely sympathetic and empathetic human. But when it comes to a bee sting and stubbed toe…no, no sympathy for you! (Spoken in the Soup Nazi's voice from *Seinfeld*.)

It's true. Lucy is very sympathetic, and has a heart of gold…which makes me wonder, Why can't I get some of that love when I'm injured?

Okay, so I know the above injury examples are a bit comical, but I have had a couple of real ones.

I fell off a ladder, which bruised my ribs, fractured a few fingers, and gave me a wound on my chin, and I haven't been able to shave for a year since. While my wife gave me slight sympathy at the beginning, that kind of went away rather quickly, and she began questioning me as to why I couldn't start shaving sooner.

I actually really did feel super bad about this one because I was supposed to be holding the ladder. Instead, I went inside to change a poopy diaper. I heard a big crash, ran outside, and Tommy was already standing up (thank God!). There were a lot of scrapes and cuts, all of which I gave top-tier first aid wound care. I was sympathetic and sorry and gave him world-class injury attention. But there is an expiration date on how long to feel bad for someone's injuries. Tommy literally milked the cut on his chin for eleven months! He didn't shave for almost a year because he didn't want to disrupt the healing of the quarter-inch cut under his chin.

The other pain incident for which I wanted some support was during my vasectomy. Yep, I took one for the team, and went ahead and got this procedure done.

It was about time you took one for the team after I went through five pregnancies, labors, deliveries, two pregnancy losses, and brutal postpartum for six years straight.

My wife's body has been through enough; it was my turn!

Truth!

Again, I AM NOT comparing this to pregnancy, but my precious family jewels were dramatically altered, and it hurt tremendously. This procedure is both emotionally and physically painful for men.

(Physically painful because you forgot to apply the numbing cream before your appointment.)

A lot of guys feel like they are losing part of their manhood, a portion of their masculinity, and then you're also talking about gleaming, sharp scalpels in the groin area. It's a lot to deal with, so I just wanted my wife by my side for this one.

I felt bad for Tommy, for sure I did. But my sympathy was masked under a bigger emotion…resentment! Here I was, weeks after giving birth to my last child, three kids under five in the car as we drop off dear old Dad at the doctor's office. I kid you not, I drove around the hospital block a handful of times before receiving a text from Tom that he was ready to be picked up. WHAT?!? That's it?! I still had stitches (again), was battling engorged breasts and postpartum baby blues, and here he comes waddling out of the doctor's office.

Now it's not that I actually wish my husband to experience more pain in his life (may we be blessed that these are his biggest injuries) but FOR THE LOVE…what we women endure and go through during pregnancy, labor, and postpartum…we each deserve friggin' gold medals!

Okay, I feel like I need to go a bit deeper here on the vasectomy because I'm not sensing any sympathy even from the readers. As Lucy mentioned above, my doctor prescribed numbing cream, which I forgot to put on the boys the morning of. When I arrived at the office, the doctor simply said, "Ouch," when I told him what I forgot to do.

He moved forward with the procedure anyway, with nothing stopping me from feeling the pain. I felt a needle go directly into my, ahem, pride. With the Novocain not fully kicking in, I felt the scissors/knife/chain saw/whatever it was go directly in there and snip some of my favorite veins. I'm not sure what they snipped, but it hurt like a mother...

TMI, Tommy...T...M...I...

(Says the woman who has brought up stitches and engorged breasts...but I digress.) I had asked for calming music during the procedure, but my meditative music was interrupted by a TIRE COMMERCIAL on the radio with a cowboy screaming, "Come down and get your tires...," midprocedure.

When it was over, I breathed a sigh of relief, but then the doc said, "It's only halftime!" As the scissors approached soldier number two, I started screaming, to which the doc replied, "Open your eyes, Tommy. I'm on the other side of the room." Which he was.

So, this was not a good experience...I just wanted SOME sympathy.

I'll end by saying again...my wife is amazing and a superstar. She naturally birthed babies heroically.

Yeah, I did!

But is it fair for her to be able to forevermore monopolize the pain game?

Alright, ladies and gentlemen, it's time for you to choose whose side you are on!

From the mom corner...After birthing humans, women live on another level of understanding pain and extending sympathy. Nothing personal, folks. Them's just the facts, and the fact is, broken toes and bee stings do not a thirty-one-hour labor and delivery make! Amiright?

From the dad corner...Women are completely selfless for allowing little humans to grow in and then dramatically exit their bodies. However, it's not fair if men are reminded of that each time they have an injury of their own! How about a little bit of sympathy?

Whose side are you on...MOM or DAD?

Are You a Hoarder or Keeper of Nostalgia?

I came to my marriage with one understanding of words, of meanings. It's taken me a while, but I've figured out that Lucy came to the relationship with different definitions for some of those same words. Case in point? The difference between "stuff" and "garbage." To my mind, garbage is something that has no potential future use or past sentimental value. Stuff, on the other hand, stuff is full of possibilities, full of promise for a coming day or full of memories from days past. I love stuff. I have trouble saying goodbye to my stuff because I worry, What if I ever need or want to see this certain item again? I can't possibly throw it away because the sentimental stuff can never be duplicated, and the everyday "stuff" could cost me money to purchase again someday.

Old wires? I probably have a few boxes full of them from old phones, televisions, DVD players, modems. What if I need a coaxial cable at a moment's notice? What if I need a three-to-one extension cord adapter? What if Best Buy goes under and sourcing electronic accessories becomes black market? What if a zombie apocalypse happens? I can't possibly throw this stuff away, because I may need it someday. You could even say it would be irresponsible of me to not make sure these kinds of supplies are always available.

True story, when VHS tapes were taken over by DVDs, my garage became the foster home for a neighbor's massive VHS library. Sure, they were throwing them away, but it gave me great satisfaction to know that I had the greatest VHS collection in town. I'm not sure I even had a VCR at the time, or if I ever watched any of them, but I was the proud owner of that VHS collection for a while. I think it was involuntarily taken away by Lucy once we got married. At least, I haven't seen them around in a while.

Now, let's talk about sentimental stuff. How do you expect me to part ways with all of my trophies and baseball cards from my childhood? Old *Sports Illustrated* magazines? I've got to keep them. What if I want to look back at them someday? My trumpet from high school? I pull it out at least every three to four years and play a scale. How can you ask me to throw away that kind of creative tool?

Lucy has a condition known as "toss happiness." It comes on every now and then, this urge she has to pillage drawers and closets and piles. You know the type. She goes into MY STUFF, and starts throwing away what she thinks is garbage. NONE OF MY STUFF IS GARBAGE! And don't possibly accuse me of "garbage picking" if it wasn't garbage to begin with. That's a classic mistake. Garbage picking would be choosing to bring home, say, a used ice cream container with a gooey layer of sugar scum cementing the bottom. I engage in "repurposing," and that's a completely different genre.

I used to keep all of the stuff from my childhood in three or four boxes. Now it's down to one. And Lucy wanted to throw out that one box. So I had to hide it from her, and it is high in the rafters of our garage, so there is no way she can get to it. Especially since I hid the ladder too.

Lucy, I gotta ask; you've got a whole house over which you blessedly exert organizational and decorative control. I'm just needing one box, one, in a dusty spot in the rafters of the attic with spiders for company. I can't help but believe that even Chip Gaines has a box or two secreted somewhere in all that shiplapped perfection of *Fixer Upper.*

I feel like I need to remind you that the garage used to be mine, a haven away from throw pillows and succulents. Then it was just a few boxes in the garage that were mine. Now the archival record of my previous life is in one box, and I have to hide it from the whims of the next "toss happy" siege. Who is this woman, and why is she trying to take my stuff away? Tell me, friends, is this too much to ask, one box perched on the dusty crossbeams in the pizza-oven heat of our garage?

I love stuff. And I will do everything in my power to keep my stuff.

You guys, this is the moment I've been waiting for. I now get to confess to the world: I legit live with a hoarder. Even Marie Kondo might need an extensive spa stay after staging an intervention with my guy. Sparking joy might just also spark some hoarder rage in this case.

I should have read the signs. They were all there from day one, that first night at a party in Tommy's apartment. It was a small apartment that he shared with another guy. Upon entering, I definitely thought, "Why do these guys have five couches in such a small apartment?"

No, that's not a typo.

Yes, Tommy had five couches in a nine-hundred-square-foot apartment.

The first couch was particularly long, taking up the entire back wall. This one was the grandfather couch; it was old with lots of rips, and judging by the worn-out material, it probably reached its prime during World War II. Then there were two love seats; not a matching set by any means, but they provided side views when watching TV. One of these was our preferred seating as Tommy sat upright and I lay over him with my legs dangling off the armrest. The fourth couch occupied the dining area right off the kitchen. Never in the life span of knowing this couch did I ever actually see a single human sit on it. Its undesirable position next to the front door, facing the kitchen, likely played a role in this statistic. Last but not least, the fifth couch was conveniently located in Tommy's bedroom. However, this full-size couch did carry some sentimental value. It was the spot where Tommy and I shared our first kiss. Unless you ask Tommy, who swears we were standing…but we were not.

Did I mention Tommy's bed was propped up by cinder blocks? The height of this bed matched that of a five-star hotel master suite… minus all the class. Under that bed, alongside those cinder blocks, is where Tommy stored all his stuff.

Little did I know what lurked within those bins and what it all meant for me.

But I didn't care. I had just met the man of my dreams, the father of my future children! And that kind of fresh love blinds you to the flashing yellow lights that should accompany a multi-mismatched-couch decor scheme. I'm talking about the kind of love that makes you know that you want to marry this guy within days of meeting him. I'm talking about the kind of love in which a couple of your nieces and your best friend are witness to your proclamation that this guy, this human you met only a few days ago, is absolutely, cosmically, truly your soul mate. That kind of love, my friends, does not have room to consider couch collections as concerning.

That first kiss was amazing, and even though I do believe we were standing; we were standing right next to that couch that I loved so much. I didn't hear any complaints that night, so I assumed we'd be with that couch for eternity. The couch in the living room with the VIP seating also holds a special place in my heart, because I remember looking at Lucy sitting on that couch earlier that same night, and thinking, "The most beautiful girl in the world is in my apartment, sitting on my couch?!?" These are memories and couches that I wanted to hold on to forever. A few weeks later Lucy and I ate one of our first meals on the grandfather couch. I never imagined having to say goodbye to that one...

First came love, then came marriage, and we ended up moving into an even smaller place than before. I had successfully talked Tommy down from five to two couches.

Then came the baby in the baby carriage. Our condo went from all cute, nice glass items off our wedding registry to all the things that come with having a baby. Cribs, bassinets, Exersaucer, high chair, Bumbo seat, baby swing, stroller, baby bathtub…it's a lot.

I started purging slow, donating or throwing away things we didn't need or no longer used to make room for our new bundle of joy. Surely a trophy from an improv group in high school or second-grade soccer would constitute as items for the "toss" pile. I understand keeping baseball cards, I have kept mine from fifth grade too…but who the heck wants a stack of two hundred plus headshots from 2002 when you used to wear necklaces, Tommy!

Wearing a multicolor small beaded men's choker in the early 2000s is the ONLY thing in this book I'll admit I was 100 percent wrong about.

Cut to almost ten years, three kids, two dogs, and one husband later…our crew has acquired more stuff than we know what to do with. You would think moving into a big house with a ton of storage space would result in a fairly clutter-free house. WRONG! There is so much crap everywhere. On every table, chair, and shelf and scattered all over the floor is an assortment of toys, shoes, hats, trash, dishes… it makes me certifiably insane!

And as luck would have it, all three of the kids inherited Daddy's hoarding tendencies. Most days I wave the white flag and succumb to the mess because spending eight hours cleaning and organizing only to have your husband and kids trash the house in eight minutes can be soul sucking.

A few months back, I spent three hours purging and organizing the kitchen. Tossing expired food, Tupperware lids, mixing bowls, sippy cups, a spatula (because surely we can go down from four to three spatulas), some mugs, utensils, and a beer stein hidden in the back of the cabinet from one of Tommy's fraternity formals in college. A stein I'd never even seen before. I left no drawer or cabinet unturned; we rid ourselves of hundreds of useless kitchen items we never use. I boxed it up and loaded it in the car before Tommy arrived home from work.

As luck would have it again, I asked him to load a bin of clothes I was donating into the back of our SUV, completely forgetting all the kitchenware that was out there. I waited…and waited…and waited some more, ultimately knowing full well what was taking so long. Finally, in walks Tommy with a mixing bowl filled with the fourth spatula, mugs, and his fraternity beer stein. I legit wanted to cry.

The weeks after this raging purge were very painful for me. I don't have time to cover all of this, but each spatula has a different purpose. One is for flipping burgers on the grill. One works better for flipping eggs in a frying pan. One works best with olive oil. And then you need a backup…

Lucy snuck some things into the trash that I wasn't aware of. For years we had the best can opener in the world. My sister got it for her wedding, and passed it down to me. Yes, it looked strange and was twice the size of a normal can opener, but THIS CAN OPENER WAS WONDERFUL. It worked so fast, so it saved me at least a couple of seconds each time I used it. I felt like I had so much strength because that can opener operated so smoothly…And now it's gone. And I'm using a flimsy replacement.

Important lesson for Lucy: You can't get toss happy with my stuff. That's my stuff! It was never garbage unless I said so. And the kitchen is my room, and we all know what. So, DON'T TOUCH MY STUFF!

Another time I was purging the baskets in our living room. One was overflowing with magazines. So out they went…Hours later, Tommy walks in with that stack of old sports magazines that HE HAS NEVER LOOKED AT EVEN TO THIS DAY!

Now let's talk about the one box Tommy claims to have left. The "archival record of my previous life in one box" as he so eloquently stated. If this were a court case, I would now present a slew of photos taken throughout our home. You see, Your Honor, Tommy may have only one box but he has successfully occupied every bench, shelf, table, and corner with his stuff. Then I would take the jurors on a field trip to his car, where they would find over a dozen hangers, pens, and enough half-opened energy drinks to fill a minibar. Then I would rest my case by tossing all of his stuff into enough boxes to fill a U-Haul truck.

So now, the only time I even consider a purge is when Tommy is out of town and the trash man is coming before he gets back. It's the only way; otherwise, my garbage-picking, hoarding-loving husband finds it and brings it back in.

It's my stuff, and I'll do what I want to. Are you even a grown-up if you don't have at least four spatulas, three memorable beer steins, and a large box full of childhood trophies?

SOS Marie Kondo

Postscript

Recently I learned a very valuable life lesson that I want to share with each of you. You see, where we live is surrounded by desert and mountains, often prone to wildfires. In the fall, the dry heat and drought mixed with superstrong winds causes fires that devastate the state of California every year. Last year was no different, only this time it hit close to home, literally. Every surrounding neighborhood was under mandatory evacuation as fire fighters fought tirelessly to contain the flames. Thousands of homes were destroyed. We watched, glued to the TV as the park where my son played baseball every year burned to ash. We waited with bated breath to see if our voluntary evacuation would change to mandatory. Tommy and I started looking around, deciding if we should start packing up and what to take in the event of an emergency. It was in that moment, looking around, that I realized it was all just stuff, things, items that didn't truly matter. With the exception of some old family photos and an oil painting my mom did for me before she died, I quickly realized that nothing else even came close to mattering as much as the health and safety of my husband, children, and dogs. Now don't get me wrong, I would be absolutely crushed if I lost my home. My heart breaks for anyone who has…but the value of life far exceeds that of anything else. As long as I have my family, I have everything I need.

Agreed. But I still miss that can opener.

Alright, ladies and gentlemen, it's time for you to choose whose side you are on!

From the mom corner…Let go of the old and welcome the new! Even better when the new is a newly organized cabinet, a newly empty drawer, a new space to hang things in the closet because the hoarding piles have been cleared!

From the dad corner…Life is too short, why not just hold on to all of the stuff that you love? Okay, sure, don't keep piles all over the house, but there should be some sanctuary in the recesses of the garage. Let a grown-up keep what they want. Just knowing the stuff of precious memories is there will make you sleep so much better at night…

Whose side are you on…MOM or DAD?

To Skydive or Not to Skydive? That Is the Question.

For as long as I can remember, I've dreamt of going skydiving.

Bungee jumping? No way.

But skydiving? Sign me up!

And in May of 2009, that dream came true. It was Mother's Day weekend and I thought, "I'll meet my mom halfway to heaven." Just two months earlier, my mom passed away from cancer. Stage 4 metastatic melanoma robbed me of my mom when I was twenty-nine years old. I knew that first Mother's Day after losing my mom was going to be heart-wrenching. So, I decided to plan something I've always wanted to do and go skydiving. My best friend and niece, Susie, flew out to join me as a birthday gift to herself. A few other friends, Kristin, Jason, and Brad, also signed on to join me!

Since several of my nearest and dearest had decided to join me for this adventure, I figured my new husband would be all in as well. Um, nope. It was a big NO for Tommy. He did not share a love for roller coasters with me, and he certainly had zero intention to jump out of an airplane with me. But he did agree to go with us and show his support while his feet stayed on planet Earth.

In addition to meeting Mom halfway to heaven, I also knew that Tommy and I would soon start trying to get pregnant. I had a small window in which to check this off my bucket list because the chances I'd go skydiving after having kids were slim to none. I will say, for the record, that if my kids want to skydive when they are adults, Granny Lucy is all in! (Yes, I have already chosen my grandma name. I'm a planner like that, and personal branding in the grandma space is important.)

After a two-hour drive into the California desert, we arrived at Lake Perris. It was go time, but before suiting up, everyone who signed up to jump had to sit through a course on skydiving. We also had to sign off that it was on us if a crash and splat ever went down. But we were jumping tandem with expert jumpers, so I wasn't too worried. Another group of my friends, the group collectively known as the "Broads," also came out to cheer us on from planet Earth. There was a pool conveniently located on the property so the Broads would sunbathe while we jumped for our lives. Tommy's plan was to hang with the Broads…until it wasn't!

If I could sum up all of my fears in the world, they would all be skydiving. Being tossed out of a plane and hoping that the parachute works. No, no, and no.

However, this was a crucial decision in my life. I decided that I had to jump. I had to go through with it. I realized that I couldn't stay on the ground. I couldn't possibly allow my wife to have bragging rights over me for the rest of my life. I couldn't have her telling my future children that she went skydiving, and I did not.

I had to protect, at all costs, my future cool dad factor.

Even with my potential paternal reputation on the line, going skydiving ended up being one of the worst decisions of my life. It was a terrifying day. I would never recommend the experience to anybody.

Before leaving the ground, as Lucy mentioned, we had to sign our lives away. Yep, if we died, our families would not be able to sue the skydiving company. They had that in writing. First time I've ever signed a paper like that. And I can tell you it does nothing to build your aeronautic confidence.

Then we got suited up and met our tandem skydiving partners. Let's call my partner Bob. Yes, somebody was going to be strapped to my back, and in charge of pulling the parachutes. Bob seemed like a nice guy, but could you really trust anybody fully in this scenario? We were going to be jumping out of a plane together! What kind of childhood did Bob have? How stable a person was Bob? Was this a hobby kind of job for Bob, or was he at the pinnacle of his tandem-partnering career? And I was supposed to just strap myself to Bob the Unknown Quantity and hurl myself, along with this stranger, into the stratosphere? Those are just terrible words to say out loud...or even to type.

The funniest part about Tommy and Bob was their opposite physiques. Tommy is six feet two inches and skinny. Bob was about five feet two inches and pudgy. Bob, if you are reading this, please don't be mad, I'm pudgy too!

Eventually, it was time to get in our airplane. Or was it a helicopter? I honestly don't even remember. It was just the worst and so scary. As we were lifting into the air, I tried to force a smile, but I felt nauseated. Once we got to ten thousand feet (or maybe it was one hundred thousand?? I don't remember, it all becomes relative at that kind of insane height), some of the skydivers started jumping out of the plane. We all had a number, so I knew that my turn was approaching. My wife was going to go after me, so she watched me suffer as it got closer.

It was fourteen thousand feet when we jumped. And honestly, the scariest part was that clunky plane with the door wide open. The thought of us getting sucked out of the plane and shredded by the engines crossed my mind a time or two.

When it was my turn, it turned into a struggle. My natural instinct was to push back when Bob was trying to throw me out of a plane, but Bob kept pushing me forward. The desire for survival began to trump my need to not be one-upped by my wife. I'm not saying I was gripping the sides of the open hatch of the plane like a cat frantically trying to avoid being dumped in the bathtub...but you wouldn't be wrong for conjuring up that image.

This is one of my favorite memories of that day. Watching the "Tommy-Bobby Tango" going back and forth. Still makes me laugh every time.

Much to my chagrin, he won the battle and we were free-falling through the sky.

I saw giant farm fields below, which started getting larger and larger quicker and quicker. I desperately held on to the cords attaching me to Bob and the parachute pack as I was certain I was falling to my death. I want to say my whole life flashed before my eyes, but I could think of nothing but what the end of that life would look like, my inert and inside-out body plowing up a furrow in the ground. With Bob on my back, of course.

I'm told most folks open their arms and enjoy the free-falling experience. I didn't enjoy any of it. Apparently, I don't find sheer terror enjoyable. I'm not woke when it comes to gravity.

Tommy and I both purchased the skydiving package, which included a videographer jumping alongside us to film the experience. Best money I ever spent. In Tommy's video, he is white-knuckling his shoulder straps, hanging on for dear life. My video, on the other hand, showed me waving and blowing kisses to the camera, so much so that I forgot to pull the strap when I was supposed to deploy the chute at the appropriate time during the free fall. Thank goodness I had a professional attached to me to pull it for me!

As the parachutes opened, we were jolted into a graceful glide. Coolest moment of my life! I was soaring like an eagle, the closest I will ever get to the feeling of flying. I spread my arms as wide as I could and hugged the wind as though it were my mom. It felt like a spiritual experience. What started out as a violent burst of chaos, feeling completely out of control, transformed into floating on top of the world, as peaceful and free as a bird.

At some point, Bob opened our first parachute. But we were still falling at a fast pace, so it seemed like everything was about to end. Then Bob opened our second parachute, and we began to glide.

I started to think that I might actually survive. Would I live to see another day?

When my feet touched the ground, I was thankful to be alive and realized that I had just voluntarily gone through the worst experience of my life. My wife landed soon thereafter. I gave her a giant hug.

Upon landing, I was quickly engulfed by Tommy's tight embrace… he wouldn't let go, actually. It was as though he just reunited with me after thinking we'd never see each other again.

Hey, Tommy, let's do it again?

Never.

Alright, ladies and gentlemen, it's time for you to choose whose side you are on!

From the mom corner…Death-defying adventure is fun for a relationship! Can I get a whoop-whoop?!?

From the dad corner…I took one for the team. Call me a martyr. I skydived so you never have to. Don't do it. It's terrible.

Whose side are you on…MOM or DAD?

Should Dad Get Rid of His Cargo Shorts?

"I love my husband. I love my husband. I love my husband," I repeat to myself as I unload the dryer full of shreds of tissues that were no doubt stuffed deep into one of the eighty pockets that are attached to my husband's cargo shorts. My inner monologue, however, has a few choice words for those shorts and the man who wears them. It's not enough to still own shorts that hit their prime the same time Britney Spears hit hers, but to completely disregard emptying the endless abyss of pockets before throwing them into the hamper. C'MON, MAN! Laundry etiquette clearly states, "One must always empty one's own pockets before disposing of laundry items into the designated hamper."

I love that you say that my shorts hit their prime the same time Britney hit hers. Dare I say my cargo shorts are now vintage?

Also, I do my best to check the pockets for tissues before putting my beautiful cargos in the hamper. But you should be doing a quick check too. That's right, the person doing the laundry should also be checking the pockets because they are the last line of defense! (More on this in chapter 13, "Should the Person Doing the Laundry Check Pockets First?")

First of all, it is not my job to check the pockets of a perfectly capable forty-year-old man's pants. For my four-year-old, sure. But not a grown man. Second, it's enough that I spend hours separating, loading, and unloading into the washer-dryer and then fold these repulsive duds that you call "vintage"…I'm not about to sift through their eight hundred pockets for used tissues.

(*Deep breaths.*)

"I love my husband. I love my husband," I repeat again as I sip wine, watch Real Housewives, and pick off tissue shavings from one thousand pieces of laundry before folding and putting them away. Because if I don't put the laundry away, they will stay folded in the basket until they are worn again and then tossed back in the dirty clothes hamper.

As you can clearly see, I have zero resentment toward my husband's cargo shorts.

There was a time when that resentment would make me second-guess my fashion choices. But sorry, my love. Most dads love cargo shorts. I've been to many parties recently where the successful, well-groomed dads are still wearing cargo shorts. I'm on the right side of history here.

I don't disagree that many dads enjoy wearing cargo shorts. And many of these dads rock the cargo-shorts look nicely. What I take issue with is the AGE of the cargo shorts that occupy our family's living corridors.

A little backstory. In January 2006, my husband and I met playing in a coed softball league. On warm California days, this handsome

Jersey boy would often be found wearing a pair of sleek, newish cargo shorts. At twenty-six years old, I found this look manly and hot…ya know, the rugged frat boy look of mid-twentysomethings clinging to their youth. That effortless "I rolled out of bed like this" look surely played a role in my immediate attraction to Tommy Riles.

Thanks for the compliment, and right back at you. I had never seen a girl playing softball in a cowboy hat, who fit into her jean shorts quite so well.

Those jean shorts are long gone and have been replaced with more age-appropriate and flattering shorts…but not your cargo shorts! The days turned into weeks, weeks turned into months, months turned into years, and years turned into two decades later…and the only thing that hasn't evolved in my guy's life is his cargo shorts. He literally, and I am not exaggerating, has had the same three pairs of cargo shorts since 2002! There was a fourth pair (camo print) that conveniently began to tear in the crotch area…so I seized the moment and ripped those babies apart clear to the hem. If I had not done this, there is no doubt in my mind, my husband would suit up those crotch-torn pants and wear them to our kid's next birthday party. NOBODY NEEDS TO SEE THAT!

Well…I love when you wear the same clothes you wore back when we were twenty-six. You mention sometimes, "I wish our relationship was like it was when we first met." Well, my love, I'm wearing my cargo shorts FOR you.

Sure, I've kept a few items from back in the day, but for sentimental purposes only. You will not see me walking around in the same clothes from two decades ago. Tommy and I have officially entered our forties and if you are looking to do something FOR me, then I would really like it if you decided to enter this decade with some style. Class it up, boy!

'Cause you know what is NOT hot?!

A forty-year-old man with twenty-year-old pants trying to look like a frat boy from the 1990s. And if you cannot let go of the cargo shorts look, at least buy a pair from the decade we are currently residing in.

So, Vote NO on Cargo Shorts!

Just Say No to Cargo!

In reality, this is so much bigger than cargo shorts. This is about any item of clothing that you love, but your spouse despises. And if you love it so much, shouldn't you be able to wear it in the comfort of your own house? I think so, yes, I do.

Now let's speak specifically about cargo shorts. They are quite possibly the most important item for a dad to own. Let's share some of the positives about cargo shorts:

- They have SO MANY pockets to carry everything.
- They often come with a free belt.
- They are SO COMFORTABLE.
- They are nice enough to wear to a family party and rugged enough to use as workout shorts.

- Since they aren't the most fashionable, you don't mind getting them dirty. And if you have kids, dogs, and a backyard like we do, you are going to get dirty. In "Should Pets Be Allowed on the Furniture?" we talk about our dogs. Cargo shorts are a necessity when you have a Saint Bernard. I don't mind getting his drool and shedding hair on my cargos!
- Did I mention the pockets? They hold baby bottles, wallets, passports, my wife's iced tea, her lip gloss, and so much more. Yep, I wear them for MY WIFE'S convenience. Dare I say, cargos are the manly version of a purse or tote.
- You can dress up and wear a nice button-down with them (depending on what part of the country you live in).
- They have lots of pockets.

Now, I can admit, there are a few negatives:

- I hold on to them for twenty plus years.
- They aren't necessarily fashionable.

But I think those negatives are actually positives! I'm saving money, and they are so comfortable around the house.

We hosted a live show in Chicago recently, and we were battling about this exact topic. I asked all the folks in the audience who were wearing cargo shorts to stand up. We had about twenty plus people standing, including a couple of ladies. When I asked the same question in Los Angeles, only one person stood up, but ALL THE GUYS had them at home.

My wife's biggest concern seems to be that my cargo shorts don't look good. When we go anywhere, everybody is paying attention to our kids and my gorgeous wife. They're not looking at me. And if they were, they'd be happy to see that my cargos are HOLDING ALL OF THE THINGS for my wife and kids! Cargos for life!

And if you're looking to sell a pair of camo-print cargo shorts, I'm buying!

Alright, ladies and gentlemen, it's time for you to choose whose side you are on!

From the mom corner…Cargo shorts had their day. Yes, their features are numerous. Yes, they are a callback to those heady days of college and carefree, kid-free years. But, it's over. It's done. How's about a nice pair of flat-front, tailored shorts? Hmm?

From the dad corner…These are the ultimate man accessory. A man's main role is to take care of his family, which often leads to carrying their stuff everywhere. He won't buy a man-purse, so his old cargo shorts are the next best solution. His precious cargos hold everything for the family, and they're old enough so when slobbered on by the dogs, his day isn't ruined…

Whose side are you on…MOM or DAD?

Should You Go by Expiration Dates?

I am a mom with three young children. They rely on me and their father to keep them safe and healthy. And last I checked, feeding children expired food is not on the list of best parenting practices.

Oh wow, she took the gloves off right at the start of this one. I'll agree with her that my main job is to keep my kids safe. With that said, most expiration dates are total crap, and my kids have NEVER been harmed by any slightly expired food or expired Band-Aids (yep, my wife will believe any expiration date out there). These companies are out to get us so we go and buy new stuff, way before it's necessary. It should be noted that I do believe in expiration dates for dairy and meats...you should take them seriously.

Well, we agree on that...but what about fruits, veggies, bread, and so much more?!

Huh? Fruit doesn't have expiration dates. When an apple goes bad after a few months, sure, we should chuck it. Are grapes turning too soft and gray? Then we should throw them away. You say adios to bread when mold appears or when the loaf becomes too hard. The key is keeping these foods until they go bad, not until somebody else tells you they are bad. I'll stand by my thought that most expiration dates are a conspiracy.

Expiration dates on food are not merely a suggestion. My children will not ingest expired food, nor will I allow their father to poison their minds with such poppycock!

Listen, a lot of these companies can't even legally say "expired by" so they go with "suggested by" or "best if used by." What does that even mean? Sure, it's best for the company if I buy new paprika because the one I have is already a couple of years old. But "suggested by" and "best if used by" are marketing terms at best. I'll keep my paprika until I feel like I need new paprika!

If by "a couple of years old" you mean twelve years, because that is exactly how old several of our spices are…yes, go buy new paprika for Pete's sake.

Would you suggest I go buy a new car battery even if the one I have is still working?

If the battery warning light came on, then yes, yes I would. Warning lights on the dashboard of your car are the equivalent of expiration dates on food. That light means your battery is about to go, and unless you want to end up stranded on the side of the road in a sketchy part of town, it would be best to replace that battery by a certain date. Last time I checked, when the low-fuel warning light comes on, you fill up your tank with gas. Boom! #micdrop

Congrats on the mic drop, but I'm sorry, your comparison makes no sense. When the warning from the dashboard goes on, you get it checked. I "check" our expired spices often, and I can assure you that they are still working just fine.

Let's dig into the real argument from our household a few years back. Lucy, who doesn't often spend much time cooking with spices, tried to throw away our entire spice rack full of spices.

A spice rack full of spices that I received as a gift from my bridal shower…in 2008! We are in the 2020s and Tommy STILL has spices in our kitchen cabinet from our wedding registry…which makes my stomach churn and adds to the many reasons why I rarely enter the kitchen.

Yes, these spices had been with us since our wedding. And they were on a beautiful spinning spice rack. An incredible carousel of ingredients for the at-home chef. We've kept our wedding rings and we've followed our vows, so why not keep our spices? I've done some research and found that spices don't go bad, they just might lose 5 percent of their flavor after a few years. That's it! They'll never make anybody sick.

Let's elaborate on this "research" you speak of…pray tell when this research took place? What are your sources? And approximately how many minutes (or seconds) took place researching said expired spices?

Look, there's even National Geographic research to back up my position. They've found spices in some of the pharaohs' tombs and have been amazed at how intact and fresh those spices were.

So, your argument is that spices stay fresh in the presence of mummies?

Listen, every couple of years I like making deep-dish pizza at home...cumin seed is a necessity for that dish. Now, if my cumin seed spice is "expired" by a year or two, do you think I'm going to go spend five dollars on a new spice, even though I'm only going to use the old one once every couple of years?

Yes, yes you are!
Because

    a) it is only five dollars,
    b) you love your wife and children, and
    c) that cumin seed sounds like it could be a dirty movie.

Let's keep the fighting above the belt—wait, I didn't mean for that to sound more PG-13. I just meant that OF COURSE I LOVE MY WIFE AND KIDS AND I WOULD NEVER PUT THEM IN DANGER. THERE IS NO DANGER FROM EXPIRED SPICES! If the "expired" cumin seed lost 5 percent of its flavor, then I'm gonna add 5 percent more of the cumin seed. NOBODY is going to notice, and they're gonna LOVE the deep-dish pizza. Also, five dollars is a lot of money! Cumin is just one of the many spices we have. You want me to go spend one hundred dollars on twenty new spices? Uh, no way.

I can just see the headlines now. "Family Party Poisoned After Father Uses Twelve-Year-Old Expired Spices in Steak Seasoning." In which case I certainly hope we don't make it out alive because we would DEFINITELY be going to jail for lethal poisoning.

Complete nonsense you are speaking now, my lady.

My fair reader, I knew you were gonna hear my wife talk a bit about how "I will only give the best to my kids, so it has to be fresh, new, blah blah blah." I'm again calling total crap. I do most of the cooking, and I will serve only healthy foods to my kids. An expired spice is not unhealthy, it's life. As the parent who spends the most time in the kitchen, I should have final say on which foods and spices are kept, and for how long.

I just want to be clear on who this advice is coming from. This is the guy who uses five-year-old NyQuil when he's sick (gag). Well, this leaves me no other choice but to wait until Tommy goes out of town to completely purge his mecca of expired spices and foods (and cold medicine). The irony is he won't even know it's gone until that one time "every couple of years" when he goes to make some dish.

Yes, expired NyQuil is fine! It's like an aged wine! Vote NO to expiration dates!

Obviously, vote YES to expiration dates.

I feel like our family will never be invited to a friend's potluck dinner again after this book comes out. And they DEFINITELY won't be showing up if Tommy invites them over for some deep-dish pizza!

Alright, ladies and gentlemen, it's time for you to choose whose side you are on!

From the mom corner…Better safe than sorry. Just throw away the dang food by the expiration date! Including the Old Spice (heh heh heh).

From the dad corner…Most expiration dates are just suggested dates, as the big companies are trying to encourage naive human beings to buy more stuff. The parent who cooks the most should decide what goes in the food. And you know this is right because there has never once been a news article about somebody being hospitalized for an expired spice…

Whose side are you on…MOM or DAD?

ROUND
12

Should You Rinse Dishes Before Loading Them?

I am so dumbfounded that people do not rinse dishes before putting them in the dishwasher. Are you the same people who think that you just dump all uneaten food in the garbage disposal? Who are you people, and where did you come from?

I knew one of them. I had an old roommate who disposed of over a pound of leftover pasta and sauce in the garbage disposal. Which led to a blockage. And then he stacked the unrinsed pasta plates in the dishwasher. He ran the dishwasher, and when the wash cycle was over, the plates were still red and crusty, and now a plumber was over fixing the constipated disposal. What were you thinking, man?

Let's define "clean dishes" for a second. I recognize that there are all kinds of gray areas in our modern life, but this is not one of them. Clean dishes do not mean dishes that have made a symbolic promenade through the dishwasher. Clean dishes are actually clean dishes!

We've all seen those dishes that have been through the dishwasher but still have chunks of food on them, almost like they have been welded onto the plate.

Yeah, you know why? Well, the lunatic who loaded them into the dishwasher didn't rinse them first. And it's not even just a rinse they need. These beautiful dishes need a slight sponge wash in the sink before being loaded into the dishwasher. You know why? Because the dishwasher is actually just a giant soap machine. There aren't sponges that go into the dishwasher and clean your plates while they are in there. Rather, it is just water and soap being moved around with extreme pressure.

Plus, where do you think all the food would go if you loaded truly dirty dishes into the dishwasher???

Now, in the spirit of full disclosure, and because I do think research can be a great thing, I just did some simple googling on whether you should prerinse dishes, and all of the columns are saying NO. Hold on, everybody, my mind is blown. Am I insane or is the internet insane? Clearly it is the internet that is wrong on this issue. Google is telling me that prewashing dishes doesn't allow the detergent to do what it is supposed to do, so my dishes might actually be dirtier because I rinsed them. What??? Is there some kind of secret agreement between dishwashing liquid and dishwasher detergent that detecting the presence of one deactivates the other, like the pill and penicillin? What kind of world am I living in here? Hold on, I need a minute...And I just read that we should be cleaning our dishwasher's filter twice a year. Man, writing this book is changing my life! I'll be ordering some new filters soon.

Honest question, does all of the garbage from the dishwasher go to the same place as the garbage disposal??

Okay, I just took a minute to take this all in, and even with all this knowledge, I still believe that if I see somebody NOT rinsing or washing their dishes before loading them into the dishwasher, I'm not certain if I can eat at their house again, unless I prewash my plate. With dishwashing liquid. In the sink.

I've been pretty quiet on this topic because the answer is simply so obvious. I'm sorry, what is the point of a dishwasher if you end up washing the dishes before loading them? Do you wash your clothes before you put them in the washing machine? Do you clean up all the crumbs on the floor before you vacuum?

You spot treat clothes before they go in the washing machine, so yes to that one.

Yes, you sweep the floor before you vacuum. What else you got?

Do you cut the grass with a pair of scissors before mowing the lawn?

Yes, you use a trimmer to get the edges.

Anyhow, you're wrong on the dishes! And Google thinks so too.

You should not have to clean the dishes before loading the dishwasher. I say let the dang dishwasher do its job and save me the time. It cost enough, that's for sure, let's get our money's worth out of this thing.

Except for knives with peanut butter on them. In that case, I wash off the peanut butter before loading the knives in, always sharp end facing down.

Convenient, that peanut butter clause.

Alright, ladies and gentlemen, it's time for you to choose whose side you are on!

From the mom corner…Let dishwashers do their job and don't bother with rinsing dishes before loading them into the machine designed to do just that. Heck, there's even a rinse cycle on our dishwasher!

From the dad corner…No matter what the articles say, you are insane to not rinse and slightly wash your dishes before putting them in the dishwasher. Be sane, rinse first to avoid stains!

Whose side are you on…MOM or DAD?

Should the Person Doing the Laundry Check Pockets First?

Many of the ways we do things around the house, we learned from our parents.

Then, at some point, we grow up and enter a relationship and possibly get married. Then you find that somebody you love may do common household chores much differently than you had been taught.

We nicknamed your mom "Mimi Poppins" because, like Mary Poppins, she is practically perfect in every way. There is zero chance I can live up to that sort of household standard.

Should we change some of the things once we get married? For sure, some we should. Everything is a negotiation to make sure we are doing what is best for our marriage.

People don't change just because they get married, as hard as one might try (nudge nudge). True story: At my bridal shower, Tommy came toward the end to open gifts with me. There was a bunch of kitchenware, specific to cooking. If you know me, you know I don't like to cook, never have, never will. So upon receiving some assortment of cooking utensils, I handed them off to Tommy, who has always enjoyed cooking. Knowing full well my position on cooking, he turned to me and said, "You'll learn to like it."

Ummmmmm, eleven years of marriage in and it's just the craziest thing...I still don't like to cook.

Now back to the subject at hand. Laundry.

One belief that I will not change is that the person who is doing the laundry should be checking the pockets.

Let's rewind a little bit. I used to get a lot of nosebleeds as a kid. It was something about the dry air over the winter. It would happen at home, and it would happen at school. One minute I'd be a normal-looking kid, the next I would look like the prom scene in the movie *Carrie*. One time it happened at school and I didn't have any tissues handy. It stays with you, that experience of having everyone at school watch you bleed out through a pair of nostrils. From that day forward, and even now thirty plus years later, I always make sure that I have at least two tissues in my back pocket.

And as it turns out, that two-tissue preparation policy comes in handy these days because my kids ALWAYS need tissues. They've been fighting off the same cold since 2011. It's snot central around here, I tell ya.

When my wife and I married and she started doing some of my laundry, we had a couple of used tissues that ended up in the wash every now and then since neither she nor I had taken them out. My wife helped teach me that I should actually be emptying the pockets before putting clothes in the hamper. And I have tried my very best to do this.

However, I believe the person doing the laundry is the last line of defense, and they should be checking the pockets as well. It's like customs at the airport before allowing someone into the country; sure, it would be best if the TSA officer and the gate agent got everyone verified before they boarded a plane. But customs is there as the final checkpoint. And that's the role of the person loading the washing machine. That person can keep tissues or loose change or ChapStick from illegally entering washing machine country. It's better for that person, it's better for the person whose clothing it is, it's better for everybody. Take the extra 2.5 seconds, and just check.

I'm doing my best on my end to remember to check; can't you offer a little bit of help here?

Those of us who are loading the washing machine? We're laundry border patrol. We'll make sure nothing unnecessary makes it into the wash. And the tissues are only the start. What if a wallet or a ring made it into the wash by mistake? What if the wearer of that laundry thought they got everything out of their pockets and then didn't? You've got to think about your family and be willing to protect everyone in making sure that nothing out of the ordinary gets washed. Do it for your family, Lucy, my love!

I'm so glad you brought that up. What IF it was your wallet, a ring, or, say, a twenty-dollar bill? You know what? If there was a chance of a twenty-dollar bill being shredded to bits by a washer, you better believe Tommy would be as thorough as a tax auditor.

When I'm doing laundry, I think I'm succeeding at about a 95 percent success rate. But that 5 percent is the percentage of times that tissues still make it through, which leads to laundry chaos, and I am blamed. I always check the pockets, because who wants a stray tissue in the washer? What a mess.

If by "always" you mean rarely, if ever…then yes, yes you always check the pockets.

Alright, ladies and gentlemen, it's time for you to choose whose side you are on!

From the mom corner…A grown person (ahem, man) should be responsible for checking his own pockets. It's not Mom's job!

From the dad corner…The (literal) wearer of the pants should check the pockets. But also, the person doing the laundry is the last line of defense. So yes, they should check the pockets too! Do it for the family!

Whose side are you on…MOM or DAD?

Laundry Limbo:
Is It Dirty or Clean?

My husband has a serious case of Laundry Limbo. You may be thinking, "What the heck is Laundry Limbo?" I would ask you to think back to that cinematic masterpiece *Inception*, in which Leonardo DiCaprio plays a man who can intercept people's dreams and discover their deepest secrets and darkest motives. But there is a danger in this kind of work. He always risks losing track of what is reality and what is a dream, what is his actual life and what is a nightmare. That's how it is with Laundry Limbo, and I would bet it lies within each and every one of your homes. You may have different names for it: the bottomless pit of pants, purgatory for laundry, debatable or undecided if dirty, unsure if a clothing items exist in a real clean state or just in the dream of being fresh. All of it shares the same definition as Laundry Limbo.

You will find Laundry Limbo on an ironing board that hasn't been closed for ten months, a bench sitting at the foot of your bed, an armchair in the kids' room, or that shelf by the front door. Always completely covered in sweatshirts, jeans, jackets, and tops, never quite sure if these items of clothing are fully ready to commit to the dirty clothes pile, but also not quite sure if it is clean enough to wear again…this, my friends, is called Laundry Limbo.

I should have known you would figure out a way to work Leonardo DiCaprio into this book, Lucy.

Next up, Ben Affleck…2002 Ben Affleck, that is.

But you won't distract me from the point: If I've worn a pair of jeans a few times, and I'm not certain that they belong in the wash, or back in the closet, I might place them on the bench at the bottom of our bed. I fully admit this is my fault. I need to be more decisive, but I'm not…

If I've worn a button-down shirt (note, I always wear an undershirt so we don't have to wash button-downs often) and I'm not sure if it's time for the dry cleaner, I might place it on our ironing board or on the shelf near our front door. I do this without discussing it with Lucy. So it probably looks like I lazily left it somewhere, which isn't entirely true. In actuality, I lazily placed it somewhere because I wasn't sure where it should go.

The problem that "unfolds" is that every flat surface in my house is now consumed with Laundry Limbo items. So instead of Tommy actually using the ample cabinet and drawer space we have, he lays his crap everywhere.

This leaves me in Laundry Limbo hell until I give up and just toss everything into the hamper so I don't have to look at it anymore!

I don't want my wife to make these decisions for me. In fact, I'm just not sure exactly what the immediate future is for these articles of clothing, so I put them in limbo. I'm delaying a decision because I'm just not quite sure yet. I need more information. However, at times, I'll pile multiple things in the limbo locations.

My wife has made the wrong decision on items in limbo in the past, and I have paid the consequences.

Oh, how I love when you accuse me of wrong decisions on topics that involve you doing nothing and me at least taking some form of action. Go on…pray tell all my wrongdoings.

Let's talk about my perfect gray button-down, which is dry clean only. I was giving it a couple of days in laundry limbo as I thought through whether it needed a dry clean or not. You can't rush a decision like that. I laid it ON TOP OF (but not *in*) the hamper. But then my wife threw it in the wash. After a wash and a dry, it has never fit quite the same. I'll still wear it every now and then if I feel like wearing a shirt that curls up in the back. Additionally, the beautiful gray has faded a tad, and it's now tight around the upper arms. It's all very unfortunate, but I'm trying to move on.

Another time Lucy made a wrong decision about a couple of items that were lying out on the ironing board. I had taken my recently cleaned suit and tuxedo out to match a couple of shirts with them, and I left them on the ironing board. I come home from work and, boom, they're gone! They had been brought to the dry cleaner again! They were cleaned two days in a row.

We need better laundry communication for sure, and I want to talk to her about it.

But first, I have to figure out the immediate fate of a couple of the items I have in Laundry Limbo. Give me a day or two to sort that out...

It's bad enough I have to do ten thousand pieces of laundry, and now Tommy wants to add "laundry communication" to the pile?! I cannot think of anything less appealing than conversations about laundry. Talk dirty to me…just please don't talk dirty laundry to me!

Just say NO to Laundry Limbo!

Alright, ladies and gentlemen, it's time for you to choose whose side you are on!

From the mom corner…There is a perfectly good place for everything in the form of a shelf, cabinet, drawer, or closet, why lay it out in the open for all to see? Clean or dirty, make up your mind!

From the dad corner…Some of life's most important decisions can't be made on the spot. Shirts get ruined if they are washed the wrong way. Sure, it might look like a mess at the time, but Laundry Limbo is helping us in the long run. Vote YES to Laundry Limbo.

Whose side are you on…MOM or DAD?

Who Should Control the Thermostat?

Scenario 1: My wife is cold when she wakes up in the morning in the winter. She adjusts the thermostat to seventy-eight degrees just so it heats up quicker, hoping to get to around seventy. Then she forgets she turned it up, and the house actually heats to seventy-eight and is unbearably warm.

Scenario 2: Over the summer, my wife is hot, so she puts the central air-conditioning down to sixty-five just so it cools down quicker. Then she forgets or leaves home, and the temp actually goes to sixty-five!

Scenario 3: Also, in the summer, my wife will put sweatpants and a sweatshirt on and then lower the AC to seventy-two degrees. Huh? Then she's sleeping with blankets and sweats at night during the summer to stay warm. On a ninety-degree summer night, you may find her snuggling under a blanket after she turned the AC down to seventy. What is going on here?

Scenario 4: Then sometimes it's the opposite in the winter...she'll blast the heat to seventy-eight, and sleep in a tank top. I like seeing the skin, but what are you possibly thinking? Summers you are supposed to be a little warm, and winters you should be a little cold.

Here's the truth about thermostats.

It will raise or lower the temp to the desired degree and then should maintain from there. They have no control over how quickly the home heats up. All they do is set the final temperature for your comfort level.

Also, I should mention, I have a unique obsession with fans. Box fans for each room, window fans for a few windows, ceiling fans, desk fans, I love them all. Instead of being an antique watch or car collector, I think I'd be entirely happy being an antique fan collector.

I think it stemmed from a childhood where we didn't have AC, just fans. It was in college (where I also didn't have AC) that I realized you can get two fans oscillating on you at the same time while sleeping. While one was cooling my head, the other was cooling my feet, and vice versa. It was a constant flow of moving air, which actually made it feel like I had invented a new form of air-conditioning. And I wasn't even an engineering major.

Now that we're talking about fans and heating/AC basics, let's talk about the temperature the house should be at.

For me, this comes down to comfort, but also money. Understand that I grew up in a house with no central AC, and my parents had to carefully watch the monthly bills. They couldn't afford the heat to be too high, and they turned the heat down from sixty-eight to sixty-two at night to save some dollars.

If we follow this same strategy in our home, we can keep the bills down, and be comfortable at the same time. Sure, sometimes you may have to put on a sweatshirt in the winter, and shorts in the summer, but this is a team effort.

Ideal thermostat settings for a family of five:

Sixty-eight is the perfect heat setting for daytime and sixty-four at night.

Seventy-eight is the perfect AC setting for daytime, and at night you open the windows and turn on the fans.

Babe, I think you switched the numbers around. I'm sure you meant to say:

- Sixty-eight is the perfect AC setting.
- Seventy-eight is the perfect heat setting.
- And unbeknownst to me, apparently Tommy got a degree in HVAC from BS University.

I also grew up in a house with no central air. Every hot, humid summer, my dad would install air-conditioning units in certain windows of the house. And we had radiators for the brutal winter months in Chicago, aka Chiberia. The AC and heat were not centralized, far from it. The whole family would migrate to those areas of the house where the only source of cold air or heat could be accessed, depending on the season. I have vivid memories from my childhood of sitting on my hands on the radiator in my plaid polyester school uniforms as I waited for my ride to pick me up. With twelve kids, it's only natural my dad watched the bills closely.

It's because of this upbringing that I *celebrate* having central air by enjoying sweatpants with the AC blasting and a tank top with the heat on. It's how I measure the generational jump that I have achieved. And no matter what season or temperature it is outside, I always need to sleep with a blanket. No top sheet will suffice. I like having both the warmth from within the blanket while sticking one leg out to give just enough heat and chill to balance my body temp.

And I have a scenario of my own for you. Picture this:

It's August in Southern California. The hot desert heat hits a hundred and four degrees and it's not even noon yet. Earlier that morning, Tommy has turned off the air before heading to work. Unbeknownst to me, I go about my day as a stay-at-home mom. The sweat begins to build in all the unmentionable areas as I put away eight loads of laundry. Now I am cranky and uncomfortable and sweating...then I realize, he did it again! And I go to the thermostat and the AC has been turned off. Son of a...(*Shaking fist to the marriage gods.*) Why? Why?? WHY???

Did I also mention I live in complete darkness? Let me start by saying our house gets very little natural light, so there is recessed lighting in every room. To avoid high electricity bills, Tommy goes around the house and loosely unscrews several of the light bulbs. Not only am I either freezing or sweating, I am doing so in a deeply dark and depressing environment.

All the money he will save on utility bills will eventually go toward therapy bills for his wife's diagnosed condition of seasonal depression.

It is REAL convenient for the spouse who spends the majority of his day out of the house to assign himself the coveted title of "Lord of All Thermostat Settings." Meanwhile, the person who spends 99.99 percent of her days in said house is left with frostbite in the winter and heatstroke in the summer.

Wait, wait, wait...the evenings are cool even during the hot summer, and the mornings are cool in our house as well because we are in the shade. So yes, in our home, we don't need AC until about noon, and then only on the hot days. So actually, I turn the AC off every night before bed and open a few windows. During the winter, it's supposed to be cold at night. So yes, I turn the heat down before going to bed, so we can sleep with top sheets and blankets. The heat I'll always turn back up in the morning to a comfortable temperature (like sixty-eight) so the kids can get ready for school in comfort.

Y'all, pray for me.

Alright, ladies and gentlemen, it's time for you to choose whose side you are on!

From the mom corner...The person who spends the majority of the time in the house should control the thermostat. Even if that means accommodating for a preference for wearing tank tops in the winter and sweatshirts in the summer.

From the dad corner...Finances have to play a role in the thermostat state of things. And there is much that can be done, aside from cowboying it with the thermostat, to ensure greater levels of comfort for the family, like the use of box fans, dressing for the season, and a general respect of the thermostat arts.

Whose side are you on...MOM or DAD?

Is It Okay to Bring a Toaster Oven on Vacation?

Picture this.

Mom frantically packing all the things for a family trip to a five-star resort in Arizona that was gifted to us. A rare occurrence since our budget falls in more of the Holiday Inn range. As a mom hoping to class up her little family of five, I meticulously packed each outfit, even bathing suits, to attempt a chance of capturing that one money shot every mother strives to achieve. You know, the one where everyone is wearing matching outfits and smiling that becomes the lead contender for that year's holiday card? I was locked in. Don't mess with Mama when she is in full-blown packing mode.

From out of nowhere, I hear a voice from the front hallway...

Tommy: Babe, I'll load up all the suitcases in the car.

Me: Aw, babe, thank you! (Reflecting on how lucky I am to have such a thoughtful partner.)

Little did I know what was about to unfold.

The secret, the ultimate betrayal, was just hours away from revealing itself.

Genius comes in many forms. For some, it's a tech innovation that changes human communication and interaction as we know it. For others, it's insight into a medical mystery that they are able to solve. Me? I traffic in Frugal Dad Genius, and, I say with all humility, this episode to which Lucy refers has a purity of genius that should not be missed. What follows is about one of the best decisions I've ever made related to frugality and food in my life. Actually, let's go a step further. This is about one of the best decisions I've ever made in my life period. Dare I say genius.

When we travel as a family, my wife packs all the suitcases for the kids, and I give her major kudos for that. My job is loading the car and preparing the kids' snacks for the trip. I like this role because it is so important if you want to keep any semblance of a budget on a family trip. Thinking ahead about food is a necessity.

If we are flying somewhere, I'll load up my backpack with food options for the family while we are traveling. My wife likes to do her own thing with food, so I'll just pack for myself and the three kids. I'm packing stuff to hold us over until we make it to a grocery store near our destination. I'm packing stuff that can be used as bribes. I'm packing stuff that would cost me five times as much at a gas station along the way or in an airport shop.

When we are driving somewhere, watch out. I'm going to be rocking a big cooler, with many options. I kick it old school, like the families of yesteryear who would pull up to a rest stop on the highway and break out pimento cheese sandwiches wrapped in wax paper. Not that I get *that* nostalgic in my presentation, but still. This past year we were taking a trip to a fancy hotel that we had been to before. I had a battle plan. I had a strategy. I knew where we were going to park, and

I knew I would be able to load all kinds of food frugality goodness into the hotel room without walking through the lobby.

So...I packed our giant toaster oven. I put chicken nuggets, bagels, cream cheese, turkey, fresh cheeses, and more in the cooler, and I was excited. However, I knew that if Lucy saw the toaster oven in the car before we left, she would try to nix the idea. To be fair, I was taking my trip-food game to a whole new level, and I could sense that appliances of this sort being included in our trip kit would seem a little, um, trashy to Lucy. But, since I was in charge of packing the car, I was able to hide it nicely, while I Tetris'd in the rest of the luggage.

My parents were going to be staying at our house while we were gone. They arrived as we were in midflurry preparing to leave. My mom was following me around as I grabbed things from the house and took them out to the car. She saw the toaster oven entering the car, and applauded me silently. I had, in fact, learned frugality from her. She asked if Lucy had seen it, and I confirmed that, no, she had not. This was a secret frugal mission.

I was so consumed, and honestly quite shocked, with the fact that we just survived a six-hour car ride with three young kids and minimal meltdowns. At home, we can't go six minutes before someone is crying or screaming (parents included). The last thing I was thinking about was the luggage in the back of our SUV. I mean, I did all the packing so naturally that aspect of the trip must be perfect, right? WRONG!

I had no idea what was lurking in the back of my own vehicle. Sitting among us, in my beautiful, roomy GMC Yukon Denali XL, was something that was about to expose me to such horrifically low standards that I would not quickly recover, but would feel the reverberations for months.

When we arrived at the hotel, I told Lucy I would take care of the unloading, that she should just enjoy the room with the kids. I unloaded the entire car and finally brought my masterpiece to the room. It was about dinnertime, so I figured it was time to just start making the chicken nuggets.

I set this sexy machine up in the bathroom, retrieved the chicken nuggets from the stocked cooler, and got to work. I stared at the toaster oven the entire time it was cooking, merrily bringing those nuggets up to a golden brown, me basking in the radiating glory of my Frugal Dad Genius. The last thing I wanted was a fire hazard...I was very careful.

The scent of those nuggets began to perfume the hotel room, the incense of my planning. My kids were thrilled. My wife was embarrassed.

Oh, I wouldn't say embarrassed even scratches the surface of what I was feeling. Sheer humiliation, rage, total disappointment comes close...Why? How? WHY? This was a gifted stay. This was a nice place, not the sort where in-room microwaves and food prep are du jour decor. We weren't even paying for the room. Surely we could at least cover the cost of food. I mean, if he had to bring a *standard* toaster...maybe. But our twenty-one-pound (yes, I weighed it) toaster *oven* the size of a large piece of luggage?! No friggin' way.

This was our one chance to live like kings, not the shanty fabulous crew we usually are. And truth be told, I love my shanty crew, but for these four days, we were supposed to be playing the part of the upper crust. You know, wear fashionable clothes that are all coordinated, eat at fancy restaurants, and shower daily like fancy families do. Not toasting our crusts back in the room. Nope. My dreams all came crashing down as the smell of frozen, processed, breaded meat set in.

I live with zero regrets because those nuggets saved us over $50 on that first night. That's right, kids' meals were about twenty bucks each at this resort, and I can guarantee that the kids wouldn't even eat it! They don't want fancy truffle rice. They want chicken nuggets.

Throughout our four nights at this resort, I'm sure this toaster oven saved us almost $1,000. If you have a budget calculator in your mind like I do, you are thinking that each $20 meal per child equals over $60 per meal that they won't like. So $60 × 3 = $180 per day. And $180 × 5 = $900.

Now, don't feel too bad for my wife. I know better than to ask her to eat anything out of the toaster oven while on vacation. She was lounging at the pool with a frosé (frozen rosé wine cocktail) in her hand as I fed the kids their "home-cooked" meals. Then my wife and I would order food from the hotel's restaurants and eat poolside.

Thank goodness for those bottomless frosé cocktails poolside… they helped to numb and drown my toaster oven sorrows.

You see, this resort had eight pools, and that is the only place the kids wanted to be during the day. I got them fueled up so they could stay at the pool all day long. And when I brought them back to the room to eat, I got a few free beers out of the deal because I also preplanned for that eventuality and had stocked up on some six-packs.

Toaster oven on a family vacation = the best move I've ever made.

I thought you'd say your best move was marrying me.

Alright, ladies and gentlemen, it's time for you to choose whose side you are on!

From the mom corner…There really doesn't seem to be a need to explain. Hauling a toaster oven into a hotel is just about as trashy as you can get. Leave the kitchen appliances at home.

From the dad corner…Kids are expensive, traveling with kids is expensive. If families don't plan ahead, the budget will be crushed. Toaster ovens fit wonderfully in suitcases and work as a parent's best friend while on vacation.

Whose side are you on…MOM or DAD?

ROUND
17

Should You Vacation Without Your Kids?

FINALLY, a topic Tommy and I both agree on! "What miracle topic could possibly cause this bickering couple such unity?" you may ask.

Well, the answer is *vacationing without your kids*. Both Tommy and I are huge supporters of this concept. So much so that we have said on many occasions how our little getaways have been marriage savers. And that's not even an overstatement from my somewhat overly dramatic self. It really has been so important to the health of our couplehood to press the pause button and escape the daily grind to get back to being the dynamic duo. Whether it is one or two nights away or two weeks in Europe or Australia for a wedding anniversary, we have found that time is paramount to nurturing our relationship on so many levels. Besides the obvious perks of uninterrupted sleep and sex, kidless trips allow you to really focus on each other as husband and wife.

At home, we are focusing on being the best mom and dad we can. Meeting demands, defusing sibling fights, calming nerves, and wiping away tears…it's loud, often thankless, and we find ourselves in a never-ending game of hot potato. "I need to shower; you watch the kids." "I'm going to get my hair cut, now you watch the kids." "The Patriots are on, now you watch the kids." (Try to guess who is responsible for that last hot-potato pass, all puns about Tom Brady aside…)

And we make it work. But it is all about them and never about us.

Trips sans kids are an opportunity to make it about us. To nurture ourselves so we can be better spouses and better parents. I have a saying: "Self-care isn't selfish." And it doesn't have to be a full-on trip away to nurture your marriage. For some couples, it's date nights. For others, it's lunch dates while the kids are in school. Whatever works for your family dynamic, just make it a priority. Tommy and I are fortunate to have wonderful, loving childcare options and we love traveling, so this is what works for us.

But alas, there is one aspect about this area that Tommy and I do disagree on…and that is how much you should miss your kids. You see, I can enjoy all of the above AND still miss the kids!

For example, let's say we're in Vegas for a weekend.

On day one I will ask him, "How much do you miss the kids?"

Tommy replies, "Zero percent."

So on day two, I ask, "How much do you miss the kids now?"

Tommy replies, "Um, five percent."

Now, on day one and only a few hours in, I'm missing the kids already at 80 percent. By day two, I'm missing them 110 percent!

Tommy, how can you not miss the kids? Our spawn? Our legacy?

Technically, yes, you should miss them. But should you miss all the things you do for them? Heck no! Making meals, doing homework, dealing with sibling fights. Do you miss all that stuff?

You see, Lucy and I are with our kids ALL THE TIME. We find a way to make it to every game, every concert, every Cub Scout meeting, and more. For our own sanity, we need to get away.

Yes, of course I miss the hugs, and the cute moments when we are away, but generally speaking, I know that I'm going to be with them 24/7 again very soon, so I just want some time away with my wife.

To keep a marriage strong, you need to reignite the fire and rediscover what it was like when you were first dating, when the priority was on the relationship and having time together. For that reason, I don't miss my kids when we are away.

Keeping our relationship strong is one of the best things that I could give to our kids...parents that are still crazy about each other and really love each other.

So, I'm saying it's okay to be a little selfish, go on a trip with your wife, and to NOT MISS YOUR KIDS.

Alright, ladies and gentlemen, it's time for you to choose whose side you are on!

We're both on the same side for this one, and we absolutely believe you should go take some time away as a couple without your kids! But we are curious...Do you miss your kids when you're away? Should you miss them? And how much?

Should You Buy Overpriced Souvenirs for Your Kids?

If my wife and I are lucky enough to get out of the town without the kids, she's dropping $100–$200 on stuffed animals, snow globes, and other overpriced items for the kiddos. It's a waste of money and time, this seeking and shopping and purchasing of what is really gullible-tourist trash.

While we're on the issue of souvenir items, can we take a moment to discuss snow globes? Snow globes, those ubiquitous orbs of the souvenir shop set. They don't say to me, "I was thinking of you!" They say to me, "Look at the awesome place I went that you didn't get to come!" And let's also be clear. In the hands of children, snow globes are the enemy. They bring so much more anger and sadness to our home than joy.

You see, when our kids get a snow globe as a gift, they claim to love it so much that they immediately fight over who can hold it and shake it, and then the inevitable happens. Someone loses their snow globe grip or someone tries to snatch said globe away from their sibling. The globe hits the floor in a blaze of mystery globe fluid and glitter, a residue that will absorb into the nooks and crannies of the grout in the tile and remain for the next century. The explosion of the snow globe renders my kids into a state of anger, followed by sadness. Every. Time.

Thanks a lot, snow globes. You cost about forty dollars each in souvenir shops, and you make our home a much less happy place.

Now, before you think I'm the Ebenezer Scrooge of vacation trips, I do think we should be getting them something. But it should be tiny. Inexpensive. The more money you spend on a child doesn't make them happier—I think it just makes them expect more. And at the end of the day, I want my kids to be excited that I have come home to them, not just that I brought them a Christmas-level haul of gifts.

When we get home, my kids are happy for a minute with the pricey souvenirs, but then it just becomes another stuffed animal or snow globe that gets destroyed.

Here's another factor that plays into this dynamic: The longer we are away from home, the more money Lucy spends on souvenirs for the kids. Now, maybe that makes sense to her, but my kids will appreciate a one-dollar item just as much as a forty-dollar one.

I still remember the stuffed-kangaroo *house* (that's right, *house*) that she bought for my kids at the airport in Australia. Not only were there multiple stuffed kangaroos, but there were little holes in their stuffed-animal house that the kangaroos went in and out of. I believe this item was over sixty US dollars. And beyond the cost, the kangaroos we saw in Australia did not live in houses, as far as I can tell. So, there's a whole zoological fallacy that's being promoted to the kids as well with this kind of gift. Imagine their future disappointment when they realize that kangaroos don't have neighborhoods of kangahouses.

Save the money and say NO to overpriced souvenirs!

Y'all, Mom Guilt is alive and well. It's a real condition that hits moms everywhere around the world. Mom Guilt doesn't discriminate. No matter our race, religion, political affiliation, we moms find a way to feel guilty and to convince ourselves that we are officially screwing up our kids big-time. So when Mom and Dad make a decision to leave their children for an extended period, that results in severe levels of Mom Guilt. The medication for such a severe condition is cured with one and only one solution…souvenirs.

Post-trip gifts, aka souvenirs, give my kids something to look forward to. When I'm not there to tuck them in at night and the tears start to well up in their eyes during a FaceTime chat, all I have to do is mention the fun gift I bought them, and the tears immediately subside. The high levels of Mom Guilt then drop significantly, and I can go back to enjoying much-needed quality time with my husband. Really, Tommy, at the end of the day, my souvenir purchases are an investment in you, so I can quell the Mom Guilt and get back to Hot Wife on Vacation status. Everyone wins when souvenirs are involved.

Babe, you're right, I do want you to stay in the Hot Wife on Vacation status as much as possible, so I've got your solution. You love Target. Let's hit Target ahead of time. Let's spend twenty dollars on ten different two-dollar items at Target. We'll hide them somewhere in the house. Whenever you come back from a trip, take a couple of items out of the bag and give them to the kids. Tell the kids the items were from wherever you were visiting. We would literally save hundreds of dollars on this.

As far as snow globes go…I now know what I'm getting Tommy for his birthday ☺

Make no mistake, I would be legit mad at you for a few days if you bought me an overpriced snow globe. And then I would give it to the kids to drop on the floor, where all the rest of the snow globes brought into the Riles house have met their demise.

Alright, ladies and gentlemen, it's time for you to choose whose side you are on!

From the mom corner…Souvenirs help ward off Mom Guilt so you can enjoy quality time with your spouse. A small cost to pay when you are nurturing your marriage, which is priceless.

From the dad corner…Don't waste money on something your kids will forget about in two minutes anyway! Say NO to overpriced souvenirs and put the money you save toward the next trip!

Whose side are you on…MOM or DAD?

Overpacking or Underpacking While Traveling?

Our kids have been flying on planes and traveling since a young age. Lucy's family is in Chicago, while we live in Los Angeles.

Once or twice a year, we head to Chicago to see all of her side of the family. Traveling with the kids has never been easy, but they always do a bit better than what we would have expected.

I'll prepare the food and snacks we'll bring, while Lucy packs all the clothing. Generally speaking, everything has been pretty smooth over the years EXCEPT FOR TRYING TO FIT ALL OF OUR SUITCASES IN THE CAR.

My lovely wife overpacks every time we fly. Thank goodness Southwest Airlines doesn't charge per suitcase, otherwise we would be screwed.

There were a couple of years for Christmas where Lucy BROUGHT ALL OF OUR KIDS' GIFTS TO CHICAGO. (I realize that I'm using a whole lot of all-caps shouting on this topic. I'm just particularly passionate about this packing situation.) I mean...that's two extra suitcases. Those gifts were then wrapped in Chicago. Then the kids opened them. Then they opened more gifts from all of Lucy's family. Then we had to figure out how to stuff all the gifts into the luggage and haul them back home.

Here's my packing philosophy for a trip. It's needs based, meaning one should pack according to a specific clothing or item needed for the trip, not a general "empty the dresser, empty the closet, empty the medicine cabinet" kind of approach that I see, ahem, some people taking.

Here are the necessities for me:

- One pair of underwear for each day
- One pair of socks for each day (unless it is summer)
- One T-shirt for every day
- A pair of running shorts (which I might use a couple of times)
- A couple of pairs of shorts and jeans that I'll wear a few times
- One or two nicer shirts or polos
- Running shoes and regular shoes

Done. It should be even easier for kids because they are smaller and there is less expected of them when it comes to fashion. So, according to my highly scientific packing math, we should need three suitcases. One for Lucy, one for the kids (combined), and one for me. THAT'S IT! Dude, we've rolled to Chicago with six suitcases in the past!

And if there is one item I can plead with Lucy about, it's this: Stop traveling with flat irons! You leave them in Chicago every time, and then we come home and buy another one. At this point, we've already accidentally procured a robust Lucy flat iron collection that now lives in Chicago. No need to bring yet more flat irons to forget in Chicago to be added to the existing collection.

Until you pack for a trip with several children, you have NO room to talk, mister!

Packing with kids is an art, a science, a strategically orchestrated plan put in place. And you know what? I think I'm darn good at it.

I first start with something easy, like pajamas. How many nights will we be there? Are we taking an evening flight that requires a PJ change? Then I do socks, shoes, undies, and sweatshirts and jackets. Again easy.

Yes, let's start with pajamas. The kids can wear the same pair of pajamas each night, maybe one backup. We don't need six pairs for six nights!

Then I have to craft the right mix of comfort and cuteness that is practical based on the weather forecast and what we have planned to do, many times requiring long- and short-sleeve options if the weather is fickle, like my children.

You are good at accounting for "cuteness." If I were in charge, I'd be looking for the most efficient route to making sure they are clothed. There's no "cuteness" in traveling with a family of five.

Next up is toiletries, which is true misery. Now, I will admit that I pack a lot in that toiletry bag, which is usually bursting at the seams. But no joke, we end up using 95 percent of what's in there. Face regimen, makeup, medicine in case someone gets sick, brushes, hair accessories, and yes, my flat iron. I will NEVER not pack a flat iron…ummm, have you seen my hair when it meets humidity?!? I didn't think so.

And, ladies, I need you to back me up on this one. Sometimes I don't know how I will feel on a trip. I may feel bloated and want a loose-fitting top. Or if I were to get sick, I'll definitely want ample comfy clothes. Same goes with heels. As much as you want to trust the weatherman, sometimes packing those Hunter rain boots is a must, even if it takes up half a suitcase. And don't even get me started if it's an extended trip with a variety of activities, each requiring a unique look. All this versus what Tommy packs, which are always the same rugged old cargo shorts and buttons-ups…even though he has really nice clothes, he chooses to look like a wannabe frat boy from the early 2000s.

Many people remember me as early 2000s Tommy. You've gotta give the people what they want!

Now, I will admit that flying with all of the kids' Christmas gifts that year was a mistake. My dad and my brother Andy had to drive their two SUVs to pick us up because we couldn't fit it all in one SUV. And by the time I unpacked, all of my beautifully wrapped presents looked like they had been through the garbage disposal a few times. So yes, all the gifts had to be wrapped twice that year.

Listen, I would rather overpack than underpack! Otherwise, there's always that one time you forget an extra change of clothes for your little one, which definitely results in an in-flight blowout, pleas to random passengers for extra Pull-Ups, and walking through LAX with one child pantsless because we don't have another pants option until we get to baggage claim. Yep, that was me…not exactly a "mom of the year" moment.

Again, the only reason we were able to even afford this trip was because Southwest doesn't charge for luggage....PHEW!

Alright, ladies and gentlemen, it's time for you to choose whose side you are on!

From the mom corner...Be prepared for any eventuality. Have outfits for all the things. Prevent having to hunt down a Laundromat while on vacation. And bring all the shoes. You want to look cute.

From the dad corner...Pack light, pack smart, and get out of town!

Whose side are you on...MOM or DAD?

Parking—The Right Way vs. the Wrong Way

My wife thinks it's best to circle a parking lot three or four times to find the best spot, whereas I would prefer to just park a little bit farther away where there is plenty of space available.

That's the reason there is so much more space where you want to park; it's a half mile away.

What Tommy isn't telling you about his parking strategy is that upon entering a parking lot, he ends up passing half a dozen perfectly parkable spots. Even our youngest has gotten on him about this. True story. While dropping her off at preschool, Tommy will proceed to pass several open spaces. And she calls him out on it! Ha ha, that's my girl!

Our four-year-old bringing this up was out of bounds! She has only driven a Little Tikes Cozy Coupe in her brief driving career. I don't think her opinions on parking should be in consideration here, given that she leaves her coupe wherever she wants on the sidewalk in front of our house. And then there's this; in her preschool parking lot, there are only about twelve to fifteen spaces. The ones farthest away from the door are only a couple more steps than the closest.

With my parking style, the car is safer, and we actually save time, even though we're parking farther away. Let me break my reasons down for you.

Car Safety

If you park too close to the store, airport, etc., there are too many cars in close proximity. Your car is much more likely to get dinged or nicked, or you could even get hit by another car pulling out of its parking spot. Don't you want your car to stay safe?

Funny you should mention getting dinged, nicked, or hit. Didn't you back into a pole in a parking structure at the airport the month we bought our SUV? (He sure did and I have proof because the evidence is still there in the form of a crimped bumper, seven years later.)

Yep, I sure did. Completely my fault. So, since then, I've started parking even farther away to be completely safe.

Saving Time

My wife will have us circle the lot multiple times looking for that "perfect" spot. She brings her own strategy to this parking vulture approach, in that she wants us to see somebody walking out of the store, and then pounce on their parking spot as they pull out in their car. The problem is we spend so much time executing this strategy and looking for that spot. And it's not just profiling for that spot, it's also then having to wait a minute or two for that identified car to pull out. We could have just parked twenty feet away, and been in the store a few minutes earlier.

"Twenty feet away" in Tommy terms is actually two thousand feet away, just to be clear.

Folks, I know what is happening here, and it is a matter of parking confidence. You see, I learned to drive in a GMC Suburban. When you grow up with twelve kids in your family, you have huge vehicles. Since I was sixteen years of age, I have driven SUVs that comfortably seat eight or more. In my teen years, I would pile fifteen people in that same GMC Suburban; it's amazing how many rebellious teens can fit inside a vehicle. When I became a young adult, I started driving four-door sedans because I was more or less broke for most of my twenties.

But in 2013, Tommy and I bought a GMC Yukon Denali XL. YEAH, BABY! I felt like I was home sitting behind the wheel of this latest edition of the vehicle of my youth. You also feel supremely safe in a big SUV versus my previous Honda Civic. Seven years later and I'm still in love with my "Sexy Beast," as I like to call her. She has traveled the country with me and my crew, often blasting Mama's favorite artist, Garth Brooks, or the kids' favorite Disney playlist, which is currently *Frozen II* and *Aladdin* on repeat.

Now, to be fair, the year we bought that big ol' Yukon was also the same year Tommy learned to drive a large SUV. His old Ford Escape was a jolly old car, but nothing can quite prepare you for navigating the Sexy Beast. And I think this affects Tommy's parking hesitations. If he goes a bit farther (aka a half mile away) he doesn't have to maneuver the driving mastery of parking the Sexy Beast that comes naturally to his bride.

Tommy may be a better speller…but I can park like a BOSS!

It's really not his fault. It must be incredibly intimidating to be married to someone so supremely capable of parking a vehicle the size of a boat into a parking space made for a Fiat. But then again, I did push a baby the size of a watermelon out of a…well, you get it. I do have a unique expertise in large objects and small containers, so to speak.

I can park that Yukon. I can. It's not a matter of ability. I park farther out of the way also out of respect to our fellow parkers. Who wants a giant car or truck squeezing into a tight parking spot right near them? I'm parking at a distance for the benefit of everybody. Aside from hearing constant grief from my wife, I believe I'm a true humanitarian in the parking lot world.

Two young kids with no idea what life has in store for them.

Parenting is hard. Hugging helps.

Marriage is hard. Tommy and I both have a lot to say. Listening helps.

A lot has changed from a couple of kids getting married in our twenties, having kids through our thirties, and now entering our forties. But one thing stays the same... my wife is gorgeous.

This is about as domestic as I get.

Lucy and I like to kick our feet out when being photographed.

This piece is called *Embrace the Chaos…* because the likelihood of getting everyone to simultaneously sit still and smile for a family photo is slim to none.

Moms have to share everything with their kids: food, the bathroom, their bed, and even their internal organs. So no, I'm not about to share my food with my husband.

My wife expects me to compliment her spray tan. Why would I compliment something that turns my wife into an Oompa-Loompa?

YOLO (you only live once)!

YOLOSWLIAS (you only live once so why lose it all skydiving)!

When Tommy and I met, I thought cargo shorts looked cute on him… But now it's 2020 and Tommy's in his forties, yet he wears the same cargo shorts from 2006.

Can someone please explain to me why (WHY?!?!) you would choose to wear twenty-year-old cargo shorts when you have the potential to look like sex on a stick? #swoon

Our engagement party… glad one of us decided to dress up!

Yep, you really could have stepped it up, Luce.

The only thing I love more than my cargo shorts is this here toaster oven.

The only thing Tommy and I can agree on…kidless trips are a must and a marriage saver!

Don't let her hotness fool you… high heels are a killjoy.

The age-old debate over real vs. fake Christmas trees. Also, one of the few battles I've actually won in the Riles household.

My wife and I have very different takes on when to break the Santa Code of Silence.

Lucy doesn't just plan a themed party she goes so hard it takes our bank account a month to recover from them.

I often like to say, "I'm a mediocre mom at best on a day-to-day basis…but I plan really good themed birthday parties! Then I take lots of photos and fill my kids' baby books with them."

"Cut your own kids' hair," they said.
"It'll turn out great," they said.
THEY WERE WRONG!

My kids will forever be this little in my eyes. Plus, my kids will grow up to be priest and nuns so no sex talk needed. Ever.

(Meanwhile, Lucy is in the next room with our seven-year-old son giving him a full-on high school–level lesson on intercourse.)

Erin Brauer Photography

I like big dogs and I cannot lie.

My girl Duchess is by far the best-behaved being in our home. Not only does she deserve to be on the furniture she deserves a throne!

Contrary to what this photo shows, Tommy and I are not always happily in love. Some days parenting is stressful and hard and overwhelming. And on days like that, I've been known to fake a symptom or two to get out of sex.

When your wife wants a serious 1920s family portrait but you and your son would rather Hulk flex.

When your wife lays out matching outfits for a family photo shoot, don't dispute it. Trust me, just do it... even if it involves you wearing a pink shirt.

I call this piece *Beautiful Mess*, which happens to also describe what motherhood feels like.

What can I say, I'm a lucky guy. Why? See above photos.

Alright, ladies and gentlemen, it's time for you to choose whose side you are on!

From the mom corner...Make your parking count. You get one thousand points for parking as close as possible to the front door of your destination, and you get five hundred extra points for guiding your boat of an SUV into the tightest spot possible.

From the dad corner...Be a good human. Leave some primo spots for the village elders. Don't crowd your fellow parkers. Make a stroll out of your parking position. Breathe the fresh air.

Whose side are you on...MOM or DAD?

ROUND 21

Is It Okay to Show Up at Your In-Laws' Unannounced?

Well, my wife came up with this topic, so my answer is absolutely, positively, YES! With my family, it's 100 percent okay to show up unannounced. I love surprises, as does my family of origin (at least I think they do). These are the people who I grew up with, and they are thrilled to see me and my wife and my kids anytime. Even though the surprise might make my wife nervous, it actually makes everybody else happy!

And with Lucy's extended family, some of them love a surprise. They would be totally cool with our crew showing up at their front door, nothing planned, purely organic. Okay, sure, she has other family members who wouldn't be so thrilled, but surprises keep life interesting, surprises bring so much joy to the people we love, and I want to be in the business of making life more joyfully unexpected.

This coming from the guy who showed up to his mom's house and "surprised" her with a bag of his dirty laundry to wash…ON MOTHER'S DAY!

Wait a second...we are supposed to be fighting fair here; you can't just throw my dirty laundry out there like that! Bringing dirty laundry to my parents' house is a totally different topic, and that day was not a surprise, it was Mother's Day! (Reader, you can check out that discussion in chapter 22, "Should You Bring Dirty Clothes to Visit Your Parents?")

My wife, however, hates surprises.

Not true, husband. You can surprise me with a spa day or trip to a nice hotel anytime.

She wants everything planned out. I can understand that, I guess, but she's married to a man who prefers to have no plans. I just want to fly by the seat of my pants (I've never actually used that phrase until now, which is a great example, in a literary way, of flying by the seat of one's pants), and surprises are the MOST FUN.

I believe there are good surprises and there are bad surprises.
Here are some examples:
Good Surprise—coming home with a bouquet of flowers for your wife just because.

I agree!

Bad Surprise—taking a toaster oven to a five-star resort. (See chapter 16, "Is It Okay to Bring a Toaster Oven on Vacation?")

This is still one of my proudest moments.

Good Surprise—throwing out your twenty-year-old cargo shorts. (See chapter 10, "Should Dad Get Rid of His Cargo Shorts?")

That will never happen.

Bad Surprise—inviting your buddies over for an impromptu game night.

Totally disagree here. Spontaneous Game Night is a great impromptu thing to do. Just inviting a few guys over to watch a football game in the garage is awesome!

You see, I have this fear that Publishers Clearing House will show up to my house with cameras and a check for $500,000. The money part is cool, but the idea of someone showing up to my house unannounced is my worst nightmare because our house is always SO messy. Trust me, it's bad. I live with mini hoarders and a husband who has selective sight and is completely unfazed by our family's "creative chaos." "Creative chaos" is a Riles marketing phrase for a house consumed with clutter and crap...literally. We have two dogs and three kids, and that math equals that there's a lot of crap. No joke, I plan the kids' playdates around the day my cleaning lady comes so when the parents come to pick up their kid they are not running for the Marie Kondo hills.

Moral of the story, don't show up to my house unannounced. It's for your own good.

When I talk about surprising family, it goes a little something like this. Think of the Fourth of July or Thanksgiving when my parents or one of my sisters didn't think they'd be seeing our family because of other plans. Since we all, unfortunately, live rather far away from each other now, I typically only get to see two of my sisters once or twice a year. Not many things would bring my parents or my sisters more joy than to see me show up with my wife and the kids.

I know for a fact that at least two of your three sisters (if not all three) would not want us showing up unannounced. Now, I'm all in for not telling the kids so the cousins are surprised. And listen, I'm not saying your family doesn't want us showing up, but they would definitely prefer a heads-up. I know I would!

Lucy gets nervous about surprising my family, but I just want her to realize I've got this. I let her make the call with things that relate to her extended family, and let me make the call on things that relate to mine. As long as we plan ahead and make sure there will be enough food for us uninvited guests, the surprise is guaranteed to go wonderfully!

And don't worry, we won't surprise them with our dogs and emptying our motor home's sewage tank into their street à la *National Lampoon's Christmas Vacation*. I have no ambition to be Cousin Eddie. We are a fun family that will add to the good times had at any party, not causing stress on our family!

I surprised my future wife and in-laws once. Lucy was in her hometown of Chicago, visiting her family. It was Christmas Day 2006. I bought an engagement ring, and I flew from Los Angeles to Chicago to propose to her. I brought along my guitar because I wrote an original song for her, and that song included lyrics when I asked her to marry me. I had called her parents ahead of time and received their blessing for our engagement. It was the perfect plan, and it worked beautifully. That's right, I surprised my future wife, and all of her family. And, believe me, everyone, including Lucy, was thrilled.

Now that was the greatest surprise of my life! BUT it wasn't a total surprise…you planned it with my mom, she knew you were coming, hence making sure the scene was set for your epic surprise engagement. You are lucky that surprise involved an engagement ring and not your dirty laundry. If laundry had been involved, my answer would have been a big fat "I DO NOT!"

Oh, the irony, my fair bride. There is now plenty of dirty laundry in our day-to-day that is the result of that surprise proposal.

Alright, ladies and gentlemen, it's time for you to choose whose side you are on!

From the mom corner…Surprise me with flowers, surprise me with a diamond ring while down on one knee, but don't surprise me with a houseful of guests who need to be fed and who might just put in a call to the health department depending on the condition of our bathrooms.

From the dad corner…Surprises keep life fun and interesting! If you are surprising somebody that you know and love (like my parents), it is 100 percent fine, and actually exciting for everybody. Take my side, please, so the fun surprises can continue!

Whose side are you on…MOM or DAD?

ROUND

22

Should You Bring Dirty Clothes
to Visit Your Parents?

When I saw that my wife had wanted to cover this topic, I knew where she was heading with it. So let me get ahead of her a bit.

My wife, my sisters, and all of the grandkids call my mom Mimi. Also nicknamed Mimi Poppins because she'll swoop in, take care of the kids, clean the house, organize the kitchen, and much more, and she makes it seem so easy. She's incredible, really. And that's how my sisters and I grew up...my mom just did it all. Just amazing.

She really is amazing. But you know what's not easy? Being the daughter-in-law to a woman comparable to a character who is *practically perfect in every way*. I can barely get one of the above tasks done in a week, let alone all at once.

Once I moved away to college, yeah, I would bring my laundry home when I could because my mom folded it better, ironed it better, and much more. My efforts in folding clothes ended up looking like the dirty pile again, and I swear the washer ate some of my socks whenever I did laundry. When I ironed a shirt, it would take a good twenty minutes and would look nowhere near as good as what my mom was capable of in just a couple of minutes.

True story. The first time my kids ever encountered an iron was when Mimi was visiting. "Mimi, what is that?!?" they asked, pointing to the iron. Yes, they were all old enough to speak full sentences when they first saw an iron.

When I graduated from college, I would still bring my laundry home sometimes when I went to visit. I believe that Mimi Poppins didn't mind doing it, that it brought her back to when I was a kid. And I certainly didn't mind her doing it. We were all good there. We had a mother-son agreement, and all was fine.

Then I turned twenty-six, and I started dating my future wife. Is that the time you should stop bringing home laundry? Maybe…but my mom and I were still cool with the arrangement. Should I stop just because my beautiful girlfriend wanted me to? In my eyes, she had nothing to do with this. I was certainly not asking her to do my laundry.

This is all coming from the guy who showed up to his mom's house and "surprised" her with a bag of his dirty laundry to wash… ON MOTHER'S DAY!

One hundred percent true story. We were engaged at the time, and his condo had coin laundry machines. So, while I totally get bringing dirty clothes to your parents' house to save quarters, this should only happen if the person bringing the dirty clothes actually does their own laundry.

And under no circumstance whatsoever should you "surprise"

someone with your dirty clothes on a major holiday, including but not exclusive to Mother's Day.

I wouldn't look at it as a "surprise." Back then, it would have been a surprise if I didn't show up with laundry. Bringing laundry home was more of a family tradition. I think my sisters did it too. Maybe? I think? Back me up, girls.

I was horrified and I fought him to the death not to commit such an atrocious gesture. His response? "She's happy to do it. She enjoys it." As a mom now for the past decade, I can safely say no mom is happy to do laundry. We do it because we love our family, but I'm fairly certain my mother-in-law did not have "do Tommy's laundry" on her list of things she'd like to do on Mother's Day!

In the end, I did stop bringing my dirty laundry to my parents' house, because I was at that point married to my wife, and she was giving me continuous grief. It wasn't worth it to me to put up with that. But should that be her call? I think it could have been a good case of MIND YOUR OWN BUSINESS.

The only "arrangement" a twenty-six-year-old son should have with his mother is to take her out to dinner regularly, call her weekly, and give her 20 percent of his paycheck each month for all the crap she had to put up with through the years.

Once I stopped bringing the laundry home, I learned how to separate lights and darks, and I even went and bought myself some detergent. Did you know they have instructions for how much detergent to use, and that you can choose hot or cold water for the laundry? Also, I found out that you have to empty out the lint from the dryer vent. These are amazing times we live in, my friends.

I'm kidding! I knew all of this and I had for a long time.

I will say once I was doing 100 percent of my own laundry, I was buying many more wrinkle-free shirts. Who has time to iron these days? Seriously. In my forties, I look forward to learning how to fold clothes. I believe in personal growth as a lifelong pursuit.

Tommy is, in fact, kidding because, folks, he only does 2 percent of the 100 percent of laundry that he speaks of. Nor does he fold the clothes. And while he does most of the cooking and dishes, laundry is not his strong suit. On occasion, he will throw his running shorts in the wash.

And sometimes my cargo shorts...

I think the proper question to ask our readers is:
SHOULD YOU BRING YOUR DIRTY CLOTHES HOME FOR YOUR MOTHER TO DO WHEN YOU ARE A GROWN-ASS MAN?

Alright, ladies and gentlemen, it's time for you to choose whose side you are on!

From the mom corner…Surprise laundry is never a nice surprise. Ever.

From the dad corner…If someone and their mom have an agreement to extend someone's childhood just a little bit, he doesn't quite understand the problem.

Whose side are you on…MOM or DAD?

How Much Is Too Much Visiting with Relatives?

I love visiting with my family. I love visiting with my wife's family. But I need to do it with breaks built in.

The thing about my wife, as you now know, is that she is one of a dozen children. A literal dozen, as in twelve. And those siblings of hers have gone on to provide her parents with over fifty-five grandchildren, and over twenty-five great-grandchildren...and growing fast. I say "over" because someone is always pregnant in this crew of hers.

I genuinely love hanging out with them, and we'll sometimes stay in Chicago visiting for two to three weeks.

But for my sanity, I need to get away. I need trips to Starbucks to do work on my computer for a few hours. I need long runs around town to keep my blood flowing.

You see, I love all of these people, but I'm not good at sitting in a room and talking for more than fifteen minutes. I need to be on the move.

Lucy's siblings all live in the Chicago area, and because they do, they have automatic built-in breaks to get away from all the reunion action. They have the perfect excuses to get away. "Got to go put the baby down for a nap. I'll see you in a few hours." "Kids need to get home early from the big family party. Time for us to head out and put them to sleep." But when you're the one staying at Reunion Central, i.e., Lucy's dad's house, you're always on visitation call.

The thing with Lucy having eleven siblings is that somebody is always stopping by! I'll think we've got a free afternoon in store, and then Lucy's niece will drop by with her kids, closely followed by a random cousin who brings along her trio of progeny. In one fell swoop, we're back up to nine kids and six adults crammed into a small living room, and the afternoon schedule becomes as packed as the available seating. It is craziness.

If by craziness you mean awesomeness, then yes, yes, it is.

Lucy gives me a hard time for "disappearing" at times like these, but a man can only visit so much!

When we are with my family for the holidays, it can be the same thing at times, and I just need to break away. A long breakfast leads into a midmorning sit-down on the couch, followed by a group lunch, afternoon tea, then appetizers before dinner, dinner, and then dessert. If I don't make a point to go jogging, I'll discover that I've been "visiting" for eighteen hours straight, which is exhausting.

Look, long visits to family are the best, but they're a marathon. And just like a marathon, the secret is pacing. I can't full-out sprint family socializing all day long. There should be water breaks, bathroom breaks, general "I can't deal with any more humanity right now" breaks. It's the secret of that extreme endurance sport known as extended family time. And it's a safety issue, because if I don't get a little moderation in all that "visiting," I might just go insane.

To know me is to know I am the queen of small talk. My husband is not...far from it. This is probably why we hit it off so well early on. I talked nonstop and he just listened until our next make-out sesh. To give you an idea of just how much chatter I am capable of, I am someone who can share my life story with a complete stranger if the line in the grocery store is long enough. I can fill an awkward silence like it's my job, both a talent and a curse. I think that's why those early years of motherhood were so difficult for me. My entire family lived two thousand miles away, and none of my local friends were having babies yet. I felt super isolated and desperate for adult conversation.

So when I have a chance to go back to Chicago for a visit, I visit! Then I visit some more. Listen, I'm only able to get home a handful of times each year to see my family and friends, so when I do, I fill every possible hour seeing someone I love. The perk about going back home is that my dad and all of my older brothers and sisters and nieces and nephews live in a ten-mile radius of where I grew up on the South Side of Chicago. Bonus, I get to see everyone!

And do you know who my family loves more than me? Tommy! They absolutely adore him. When I book a trip home, the first question everyone asks is, "Is Tommy coming?" I don't mind. He is pretty fantastic. (Just don't tell him I told you.)

But, like our kids, Tommy expires...quickly. I will be sitting there chatting with my niece Susie, my best friend, while our kids play. When you are the youngest of twelve kids, you grow up with your nieces and nephews as your playmates and peers. Suddenly out of nowhere, Tommy pulls a Houdini and disappears. No one actually sees him leave either. He's there and then after a few minutes POOF, he's gone. Now, truth be told, this disappearance act usually happens around the time Susie and I start talking about graphic female anatomy or some annoying postpartum symptom.

POOF! He's out.

Okay, let me explain this disappearance a bit. First off, I'm doing it out of respect. I don't want to break up the convo that Lucy and her niece are having about who knows what. Second, I don't want to have a conversation about why I'm going upstairs or what I'm about to do. It just adds an unnecessary layer of complexity to a simple action of taking a social breather. At night, there is not even an option to say good night at my wife's family parties. If I do, I start getting guilted about staying up and having one more beer. And listen, I enjoy that one more beer, but then there is always another, and another. Somebody's gotta wake up with the kids in the morning! Thus, I started following in the footsteps of Lucy's ancestors, and pulling off the Irish goodbye, which is defined as the following: when you sneak out of a party without telling anyone. It may seem rude, but it keeps you from having any awkward, half-in-, half-out-the-door conversations. So, you could argue here that I'm simply keeping up with the family cultural roots.

I'm okay with Tommy's take here. I get it. Lord knows I step away, usually to nap with my youngest, when I'm with my in-laws. But I do think Tommy needs to expand his visitation time limit. Fifteen minutes is way too short for visits with relatives we rarely see.

I'm happy to hang out with family for hours! But just sitting on a couch or at a table and talking for more than fifteen minutes? I just can't. Let's head to the backyard and have a beer while watching a football game. Now, that's the type of visiting I can do for a while.

A suitable family visit should be at least forty-five to sixty minutes. An hour is more than reasonable, coming from someone who can talk for four hours straight.

No, I'm not exaggerating. I have proof.

A few years back, three of my sisters, Jeanie, Mary, and Geri, met me in Las Vegas to go see Shania Twain. After a super-fun trip to Sin City, my sisters extended their trip and drove back to Los Angeles with me to visit with my crew. Road-tripping with my sisters, kid-free, was a little slice of heaven! We talked and talked and talked…at least that is how I envisioned it. Then, about fifteen minutes before arriving back to my house in LA, my sister Geri turned to me and in the nicest way possible said, "Lucy, do you realize you haven't stopped talking this entire car ride?"

It was a four-hour drive.

"What?! Why didn't you call me out sooner?" I yelled.

I was mortified. How selfish could I be to completely monopolize a four-hour car ride without even realizing it? I legit wanted to muzzle myself.

That's when my oldest sister Jeanie chimed in. "We just thought you needed to talk. Being away from all of us must be really hard. You obviously had a lot to catch us up on."

Thank you, God, for sisters! Seriously, they are the best. I could cry. And she was so right. At that time, I was a full-time stay-at-home mom with three kids under the age of six. Our own mom had died three months before I became pregnant for the first time. I questioned everything I did, always thinking that I was doing this mother gig all wrong. I rarely, if ever, left the house. So, the only people I talked to were my kids and my husband, who believes a fifteen-minute visit is enough! A four-hour verbal sister soul baring was medicine.

In other news, if any radio stations are looking to hire people who can talk to themselves for four hours straight, I'm your gal!

The girl can talk. No doubt about that. But then so can her niece Susie, her nephew Pat, her nephew Andy...That's why sometimes you just have to "disappear." I love you, but good night. My ears are tired.

Alright, ladies and gentlemen, it's time for you to choose whose side you are on!

From the mom corner...Visit your family. Connect. Do not be controlled by the tyranny of the clock. Enjoy your people.

From the dad corner...Family should be celebrated, but in the right doses. There are times that one needs to step away from the small talk for someone's own sanity. And let's not ignore the beauty of an Irish goodbye.

Whose side are you on...MOM or DAD?

Christmas Trees:
Real vs. Fake

There is nothing quite like the thrill of waking up Christmas morning to the smell of pine coming from your living room. You carefully remove present upon present from beneath the pricks of pine needles, a gentle reminder that you are in the presence of Mother Nature.

This is what children raised with real Christmas trees carry in their hearts throughout life.

My mom always felt bad for the ugly trees. You know, the ones missing branches with gaping holes that you would have to hide by positioning it facing the wall. My mom felt like no one would pick these particular trees, and she didn't want them to be alone come Christmas morning. And so, my dad would load up a "Charlie Brown" Christmas tree into the van year after year. Once adorned with tinsel, big colored bulbs, and handmade ornaments, it would stand proudly beaming out the front room window. It acted as a night-light, staying on for two weeks until the needles began to wilt. And for that moment in time, a brief two weeks, our living room smelled of fresh pine and true Christmas spirit.

Cut to today; gone are the days of pine-filled nostalgia. That was all ripped from my memory a few years back when I succumbed to my husband's idea of "practical plastic." I cannot speak of it, only to say it comes in a box instead of grown from within Mother Nature's earthly loins. It is broken into pieces mounted on a metal stand in lieu of sturdy bark. It carries no scent...only a vacant pit of emptiness.

Innovation. I believe in innovation. Cars, bionic arms, and computers are advancing faster than we could have ever imagined. So are fake Christmas trees. Let's embrace change, especially during the holiday season.

My family, too, had a real tree throughout some of my childhood, but we eventually learned that Christmas isn't about real trees...it is actually about love and giving to others.

In all honesty, I think my parents wanted to keep a tree up for longer than two weeks, so for the second half of my childhood, we switched to a fake tree. With a fake tree, you can extend the season of love and giving for an additional two to four weeks!

When I was a kid, I remember my parents always talking about how they found it funny that when a real tree was so nice, people would wonder if it was fake. And when my parents tested a fake tree one year, everybody thought that it was real, since it looked so good. We were Team Fake Fir for the rest of the way. Plus, it saves you money and hassle!

You're gonna laugh at this, but some of my favorite memories were taking the color-coded branches out of the box, and building our fake Christmas tree each year.

It was exciting to take the largest branches out of the box first and load them into the lowest part of the fake trunk. Then we'd place the medium branches up a little bit higher, and the smallest branches up top.

My sisters and I would have a little assembly line of taking the branches out of the box and putting them up on the tree.

The process was equally exhilarating and relaxing when we had to start massaging the branches as the fake needles became fuller. With the perfect touch as your fingers rotated over the branches, it seemed like the tree actually started coming to life. I swear, I smelled pine one time as I was doing this process. Somewhere, deep inside this fake tree, was some pine.

Now, back to the innovation. Today's innovative fake trees go one step further—often the lights are already built in, so you can just connect the tree and plug it in. Really, the only complex part of putting up a tree is figuring out where to put the decorations. And I leave that up to my wife.

She's very particular about the decorations, so we just let her have her way. We actually have TWO fake trees now, one that my wife decorates and one that the kids do. Nobody in the world would get two real trees, so again, fake trees are the winner in this scenario.

And let's not forget, cleaning up after a real tree is a vacuum-clogging, combustible-needle-cleaning hassle. Real trees leave behind a biosignature that ensures you keep finding Christmas evidence far into the spring. So, I could argue that fake trees are also more...hygienic.

Lucy spoke earlier about loving the smell of fresh pine. Easy hack, get a pine-scented candle, and light it next to a fake tree! Then you can smell pine whenever you want.

Finally, to hammer down the best reason for fake trees, you can keep them up for longer! My wife IS Christmas, and deep down she LOVES to have our TWO Christmas trees up from November 15 to January 15. That ain't happening with real trees.

Vote for fake trees, and your Christmas will (1) be less expensive, (2) be easier, (3) last longer, and (4) be vegan. (Okay, that last one is a stretch, but still...)

FAKE TREES FOR LIFE!

Vote for REAL CHRISTMAS TREES if you, too, enjoy savoring the true senses of Christmas; pine, bark, needle pricks, and pure joy!

Alright, ladies and gentlemen, it's time for you to choose whose side you are on!

From the mom corner...When it's the most wonderful time of the year, it's also time to celebrate with things in your home that are wonderful. And it doesn't get much better than a real tree, with the scent of the season wafting throughout the house. Christmas isn't about convenience; it's about real laughter, real joy, and yes, a real tree.

From the dad corner...When you've got three kids and two dogs (or more), simplicity is what always works. You can't beat the convenience of keeping a tree in a box, and you've gotta love that you can extend the Christmas season with a fake tree, allowing the tree to be set up in November and to stay up until whenever the mood hits you to take it down. The nostalgia surrounding a Christmas tree stems more from putting ornaments on the tree than the tree itself.

Whose side are you on...MOM or DAD?

ROUND

25

Should You Respect the Santa Code of Silence?

I believe in the magic of Christmas. I'm your guy. I'm a Christmas lifer. Bring me all the Christmas cheer, bring me eight tiny reindeer. So committed am I to the magic, so committed is the family I come from that when my sisters and I were in college, we were still getting gifts from Santa under our fake Christmas tree.

Thinking back to my childhood, there was absolutely nothing better than Christmas morning. That awe of running down the stairs from my bedroom to see the presents in front of the Christmas tree. Santa would always get us each a few small gifts and then one big family present.

The big family gift that I'll remember for the rest of my life was when Santa replaced our living room table with a pool table! The joy I had knowing that I'd be playing pool for the foreseeable future was amazing. And again, think of the commitment to Christmas magic, allowing the family dining table to be replaced with the training ground for an up-and-coming pool shark. That's Christmas commitment right there. Santa had the ability to give us incredible gifts, gifts that I didn't think my parents could afford. Santa was a hero, and we were so thankful for him.

When I was in fourth grade, I learned the truth about Santa Claus, that catalytic coming-of-age moment where the knowledge that parents have been involved in the Santa game is exposed. I was shocked. And I was also now armed with dangerous knowledge. I'm not proud of what I did next. I went home and told my younger sisters. Yes, I took a fragile portion of their childhood and crushed it under my older-brother heel. They cried. Whatever my reasoning was, it just seemed like the thing to do. But I think I knew then, and I still know now, that I was wrong to do it.

Fast-forward to today. Our daughter Babs is ten, our son Tommy is eight, and our youngest daughter Katie is five. My wife was driving them around somewhere when a question about Mr. Claus came up, and I found out later that she confirmed to our oldest the truth about Santa.

Immediately this made me think; isn't that something that you discuss with your partner *before* having that conversation? Christmas and Santa are so important to this family, so let's talk that one out a bit, I say, before we disclose how the Santa sausage is made.

I fully realize that, in my earlier life, I messed this one up by telling my younger sisters, so this time I want to keep the magic alive as long as we possibly can! I'm a changed Santa CIA man, and there are some things the younger public simply doesn't need to know just yet.

Let me start off by saying no one loves Christmas more than I do. NO ONE. Especially not my husband, who, though he claims to have Christmas love in his heart, sometimes seems a bit more OG. You know, Original Grinch, the grumpy one, before Cindy Lou Who helped grow his Grinch heart three sizes and he took on the "strength of ten Grinches plus two." I have a name for myself during the holidays, and that is Sister Christmas. I love the spirit of Christmas, I love celebrating the birth of Jesus, I love the Christmas lights and decorations, I love the season of giving, I love absolutely, positively all of it!

I know I'm gonna get flak for saying this, but when my ten-year-old child asks Mommy a smart, thoughtful question, I answer truthfully. (See also our the birds and the bees topic: "When Is the Right Time to Talk to Your Kids About Sex," chapter 33.) One of the most important things I can do for my kids is give them 100 percent transparency and access to me. I want them to know that they can ask and tell Mommy anything.

When our son was a toddler and could barely talk, he asked Mommy to bring him his Easter basket because he was afraid of the Easter Bunny. I happily obliged. And rightfully so, because some of those bunny costumes are downright terrifying.

And when Mommy and Daddy kept forgetting to leave a dollar under our kids' pillows from the Tooth Fairy, our kids caught on. They realized that as soon as they reminded Mommy and Daddy about the missing dental payment, the Tooth Fairy would suddenly remember and show up with a motley collection of change and bills. Once they were onto us, I ended up showing them my sock drawer full of Ziploc baggies with teeth in them.

Now, Santa is a different category for me. I would have loved to keep the Santa-secret game going for as long as possible. As a child, I loved the concept of jolly old Saint Nick delivering gifts to me on Christmas morning. But when I was about six, I remember lying in bed one Christmas Eve realizing I had never kissed my mom good night. Wanting to stay on the good list, I hurried down those drafty hardwood floor stairs, and before I reached the mid-staircase landing, I saw my mom wrapping presents while my sister Geri filled the stockings. I turned around and went back upstairs, understandably disappointed. Knowing the truth about Santa way earlier than any of my friends was not an easy secret to keep, but I did not tell, not even my mom, that I had uncovered Santa's secret identity.

With that Santa background, jump to my life today, and here is how the incident Tommy was describing with my daughter went down. We were driving home from the mall in July, not even close to the holiday season. My youngest was begging for some toy she saw at the mall, to which I replied something to the effect of, "I don't know, maybe Santa will get it for you for Christmas." My oldest sat quietly in the way back of the SUV, pondering my reply. And I could feel it coming, even before she opened her mouth, that my oldest daughter was about to subject me to the Santa Third Degree.

The following is the unofficial transcript of that query:

Babs: Mommy, is Santa even real? How does he fly around the world in one night bringing toys to every kid? How is that even possible?

Me: (*Inner monologue.*) Oh crap, what do I say? She's not a toddler. She's almost ten. Think, Lucy, think.

Just then I caught a glimpse of my daughter in the rearview mirror. Her face said it all. This was the moment. This was when the next level of mother-daughter trust would be built…or wouldn't.

Me: You know what, Barb, no.

Babs: (*Most likely expecting me to lie.*) No?!?

Me: Nope. Let's talk when we get home.

Somehow the other two kids in the car remained completely oblivious to our conversation. This would make for the one time that I didn't mind that they weren't listening to me.

When we finally arrived home, Babs and I walked into my bedroom, where I could give her more of the Santa DL away from her younger siblings. I hugged her with excitement and reassured her that now she would get to be Santa with me and Daddy and she would share in the magic of giving. I let her know that Santa was not one single man in a red suit. He was a symbol for giving to those you love without recognition, similar to the way Jesus gave His life to us.

She got it. She wasn't sad; actually, everything suddenly made much more sense to her. She was all in to be a part of the magic. She didn't pull what her dad did and immediately tell her younger siblings the moment she knew. She actually hasn't told anyone, which is impressive because she is super close in both relationship and age to her brother.

Now she gets to shop for Christmas gifts on Black Friday with me, she gets to stay up late and stuff the stockings after the littles go to sleep. Adopting a new Santa tradition can be just as magical.

And do you know what I learned? Christmas morning was STILL magical after Babs's Claus revelation. It still is to me today, and I'm the one wrapping and putting out the gifts. Why? Because Christmas is not about Santa, and he isn't what I've raised my kids to think it's all about either. In our family, Christmas is about Jesus and being together with family, sharing and giving joy to one another. Sure, the Santa gig is fun when you have little ones; I still have a few that believe, and it doesn't change a thing now that my oldest knows. The only thing that stays consistent is that my children know they can ask Mommy anything and I will be honest and truthful.

Will my Babs still receive gifts from "Santa" under the tree? For sure.

Will my kids still receive gifts from "Santa" when they are teenagers? One hundred percent.

And don't forget about when they're home from the holidays from college. Santa should still give gifts then too.

Alright, ladies and gentlemen, it's time for you to choose whose side you are on!

From the mom corner…Once one of the kids asks, it's time to tell. As discreetly as possible with other kids around, but still.

From the dad corner…Keep the secret alive as long as we possibly can! Christmas is the best time of year, and you want to keep it as magical as possible for the kids. In this instance, don't tell the truth!

Whose side are you on…MOM or DAD?

Should You Pretend to Like Gifts?

"I got it! I finally cracked the code and know exactly what to get my husband for his fortieth birthday!" I thought to myself.

You see, my husband is one of those people who are impossible to shop for. He doesn't like when I spend money on him, and he's super particular when it comes to what he likes and doesn't like. For example, if I pick out a nice button-up shirt for him, I end up buying four shirts total knowing full well I have a one-in-four chance of him actually keeping it. Same goes with shoes, pants, ties, and shorts because this is the guy that is perfectly content wearing his twenty-year-old cargo shorts (see chapter 10, "Should Dad Get Rid of His Cargo Shorts?") and returning any other shorts options I attempt to pick out. For the love...

But not this time. I have finally figured out just what to get him. He is going to LOVE it! How could he not, right?! I'm not even going to give him a hint. It will just arrive the week of his fortieth birthday and cause such immense joy and approval that he will wrap me in his warm, manly embrace and kiss me like a sailor home from war.

I love your hope for the kiss like a sailor home from war. With Christmas approaching as I write this, I will make sure to give you that treatment for one of the gifts you give me. You are awesome, my love, so I want to give you that embrace.

However, I'm not a very good liar. Never have been, and I'd like to believe that I don't lie about anything…I'm a straight shooter. What you see is what you get. With that being said, I have no choice but to react appropriately when I don't like a gift.

There are certain gift-giving and gift-receiving rules to follow. For example, the appropriate way to react to a gift you don't like is to NOT tell the gift giver you don't like it. As Stephanie would say in *Full House*, "How rude!" The polite thing to do is to find something positive about the gift, thanking and nodding along at how much you appreciate the item. You can do this for virtually any gift. For example, at my baby shower, I received two baby bathtubs from two different people. When I opened the first bathtub, I was clearly thrilled, envisioning bathing my little lady in there. So, when the second tub came along, I didn't want my other friend to feel bad because I had already received one, so I reacted equally as thrilled. "This is so perfect! Now I have a tub to keep at my in-laws' home when we visit! Thank you SO much!"

Now that is how you receive a gift. Even if you fully plan to return, exchange, or regift it. You receive a gift knowing that this person put forth an effort to think of you. People want to feel appreciated, and they want their generosity acknowledged.

I seriously struggle saying, "I love it," or, "This is great," when I know that I will never wear those skinny jeans. I can't put a big smile on my face when I know that a gift was bought for me that cost the gift giver way too much money! I just feel terrible, which I guess is why I don't really want gifts. I don't want people spending money on me when I never needed that item in the first place.

My biggest struggle? Since Lucy and I split a bank account, if she gives me a gift that I believe we can't afford, I have trouble pretending that I love it.

So, what am I supposed to do? Never buy my husband another gift again? I would feel like the worst wife on the planet. It is also worth noting, no gift I give breaks the bank or is over our budget. I pay the bills, so I'm acutely aware of our finances. And while I admittedly love a brand name, if I'm the one buying it, that brand-name item likely came right off the Marshalls or HomeGoods sale rack.

What can I say, I love giving gifts. Personally, I believe in the ideal that it is in giving that you receive. Not surprisingly, my "love language" is giving and receiving gifts. It is literally how I show my love!

Well, since you brought up love languages, when you are gifting, shouldn't you do what the other person's love language is? Mine is acts of service. Put in the work to make me the tastiest burger for my birthday, and I'm a happy camper.

So here I was, the week of my fortieth birthday, when a large and heavy package arrived. My wife had gifted me a "beer of the month club" membership! I totally understand where she was coming from. I love beer, and I can see why she would think I'd be excited by this.

And there was initial great excitement as I was opening up the box to see what types of delicious brews were inside. But when I saw the beers, they were all dark beers. I like a lager or a pilsner; these were brown ales and such, which I don't care for. So, I couldn't help but ask what the monthly fee was, and Lucy said, "Forty dollars."

Yes, forty dollars a month for your fortieth birthday in the form of your most beloved indulgence of all time...beer. Ummmm, you're welcome!

Okay, so then I couldn't help my mind from heading into calculator mode. Forty dollars divided by twelve beers equals over $3 per dark beer, which I would struggle to drink. I could go to the grocery store and get a twelve pack for only $10.

Meanwhile, here we are trying to cut down on cable bills, and now another $40 per month has appeared as a "gift."

Stop talking about the cable bill, we are not getting rid of Bravo and E!

Have I mentioned I know I'm wrong in doing all this thinking in real time when my wife was trying to be kind by giving me a gift? But my calculator brain doesn't stop there. Okay, $40 per month times twelve months equals $480 for a year of a gift for me? And now I have to call them and tell them please don't send dark beers...do I have that type of control?

Anyhow, I'm certain I handled this wrong, but I asked my wife what the cancellation policy was like, and she said, "Well, you can't cancel for the first three months without a penalty"...Wait, what?

Fast-forward to a week later—I was stressed all week about this. I had to pay an extra $20 for early cancellation, so my gift was $60 for twelve beers I don't want to drink. I'm a jerk. Sheesh.

Happy fortieth to me.

You know what, Tommy? I KNOW you enjoyed your fortieth birthday. You were in Vegas with "Vacation Lucy" and she did not disappoint, if you know what I'm saying.

You're welcome.

The best gifts I gave Tommy that he did not return...

- Tickets to his first-ever Patriots game in Indy against the Colts, hotel and flight booked
- Tickets to the Bears game while visiting Chicago for Christmas one year, making it his first-ever NFL game
- Tickets to an Angels game where his whole family surprised him in the tailgating parking lot

Those gifts were awesome! I do love family surprises (which we talk about in chapter 21, "Is It Okay to Show up at Your In-Laws' Unannounced?").

The best gifts Tommy gave me that I did not return...

- An engagement ring

Lucky for him I didn't decide to ask what the cancellation policy was on this gift.

Alright, ladies and gentlemen, it's time for you to choose whose side you are on!

From the mom corner…Just be grateful for the thought. Go along with the gift giver. Be happy. Drink the beer that is handed to you!

From the dad corner…Honesty is important in every aspect of this life. And this includes receiving gifts. Don't lie to someone's face if you know you'll be returning that gift for store credit. And any gift with a monthly fee on the family's credit card is actually not a gift at all, even if they are delivering beer to your doorstep.

Whose side are you on…MOM or DAD?

ROUND
27

Which Holidays Require Gifts?

I simply love the holidays. All of them! The excitement I feel when I stroll through the aisles of Target after they've restocked the shelves with the newest holiday decor (I'm a total sucker for that three-dollar section). The thrill that my littles ones exude as they anxiously await the upcoming holiday. And I'm not just talking about Thanksgiving and Christmas holidays, I'm talking about Valentine's Day, the Fourth of July, all of them!

It is simple. Here are the holidays that require gifts for my family:

- Birthdays
- New Year's
- Valentine's Day
- Saint Patrick's Day
- Easter
- Mother's Day
- Father's Day
- Last Day of School
- Fourth of July
- Wedding Anniversaries
- First Day of School

- Halloween
- Thanksgiving
- Christmas

Let's start with a positive. My kids get SO EXCITED for every holiday. And it's because they know they are going to get a special treat. They know these gifts come from their mama, and they love her so much.

That said, I can't not say this. What Lucy wrote above is one of the most stressful things I have ever read. I mean, I know you buy little (and big) gifts for the kids on these occasions, but to see these "requirements" in writing is making my blood boil. There's something about it that feels so compulsory. But I want to give Lucy the chance to persuade me, so, my love, why don't you go ahead and explain to all of us your overgenerous gift-giving reasoning and strategy...

I'm glad you asked!

Birthdays are that one day a year that is truly your own. There's usually a party, presents, or an unforgettable experience planned. For my kids, I go all out with themed birthday parties. They now know to request their theme well in advance so that I have time to get my Pinterest on. I've been known to plan birthday parties with themes such as "Solar System," "Backyard Campout," "Planes, Trains & Automobiles," "Construction Site," "Amusement Park," "Somewhere Over the Rainbow," as well as the tried-and-true "Frozen," "Dinosaur," "Puppy," and "Minnie Mouse" themes. I often say to people, "I'm a mediocre mom on a day-to-day basis...but I throw really great birthday parties!"

You literally throw the best birthday parties. (To self: *Okay, bite your tongue, don't talk about how much these parties cost...*)

New Year's includes some poppers and sparklers, maybe some pots and pans to bang together if we stay up past midnight. Definitely not a holiday I spend much time gift giving.

Phew. Because, we just spent soooo much on Christmas.

Valentine's Day requires something sweet like chocolates and a snuggly stuffed animal for the kids. For the hubs, there is usually a card with something sexy to go with it. And I personally enjoy flowers, as overpriced as they are.

We have over two hundred stuffed animals in our home, no joke! Just saying. And yes, please on that "sexy" gift for me. That is a gift about which I am very "pro."

Saint Patrick's Day is corned beef and cabbage paired with Guinness for the adults and some gold chocolate coins and leprechaun treats for the kids. My Irish heritage also requires some festive Saint Paddy's Day decor.

I'll drink to that!

Easter is for all of us Christian folks who celebrate the Resurrection of Jesus. It starts with the search for the little ones' baskets full of treats. Then mass followed by an Easter egg hunt. I like to give outdoor gifts for this holiday—chalk, jump ropes, kites—because the weather is warming up and it's the perfect time to play outside. I admit, one year I went overboard and bought my three-year-old a Peppa Pig bike. But it was on clearance when Toys"R"Us was going out of business.

So, growing up we had chocolate in our baskets...our kids get gifts in their baskets...or bicycles with baskets...

Mother's Day is all about mom for once. And we moms deserve all the things!

You are the best, and you deserve all the mom things!

Father's Day is all about the dads who also deserve all the things!

I just want a beer and a burger!

Last Day of School is usually a small gift or treat. Recently, I've been blowing up some balloons and writing some sort of congratulatory message on it followed by ice cream or some type of treat. School is hard, and I want my kids to know all their efforts over the past nine months are acknowledged.

Fourth of July will usually include some glow sticks, flags, poppers, and patriotic apparel. Not so much gifts as little crafts and activities to do. This is when the three-dollar Target aisle is clutch!

Wedding Anniversaries are a big deal, about as high in importance as birthdays, if not more so. It's because you have another year of marriage under your belt, that for another year, you've beaten the odds. Marriage has its challenges, challenges over daily life, challenges over decisions big and small, challenges of living with someone different than you. Heck, even this book clearly shows all of the differences in my and Tommy's marriage. It's twelve months of loving, fighting, bickering, crying, and laughing together. Instead of a gift, Tommy and I usually use this milestone to do some type of experience together.

This was a great idea. We started doing something for us that made us both happy. No pressure of gift giving for once! And we have lived it up on these anniversaries and made some great memories.

First Day of School is the excitement of your kids as they pick out backpacks, school supplies, lunch boxes...all new, for the new school year. But the real gift of back-to-school lies within the hearts of every parent as their inner monologues quote William Wallace in *Braveheart* as they yell, "FREEEEEEEDOM!" after dropping their kids off at school.

Halloween is when the three-dollar section at Target does it again, providing fun little crafts and activities for the kids to enjoy as they anxiously await the night of pure sugar indulgence!

Um, it should be noted that I believe you bought Halloween costumes at Disneyland for one or two of the kids this past year. I mean, could we possibly pay any more for a costume? I dressed up as Davy Crockett for the majority of Halloweens in my childhood. That purchase of one coonskin cap probably saved my parents hundreds of dollars on other costumes for me throughout the years.

Thanksgiving: I know this is going to sound shocking after reading all of the above, but I actually don't give gifts for Thanksgiving. I donate food to food banks.

You are the most generous person I know, in many ways!

Christmas is my jam. To know me is to know I love Christmas. I've even given myself the title of "Sister Christmas" because I am all in from November 1 to January 6! Each year, I give my kids more gifts than I received in my entire childhood. I think it's partly because I was the youngest of twelve kids and so I didn't get a ton of gifts. And it's partly because I collect gifts throughout the year for Christmas, so by the time December rolls around, I've got stock to get out to the Christmas factory floor, so to speak. And no, it's never too early to start listening to Christmas music.

Moral of the story, giving gifts is my love language!

Okay, enough little quips by me; here's my full take. Holiday gifts stress me out. And when it comes to getting gifts for my wife, it is the triple whammy. Christmas, her January birthday, and Valentine's Day all come within two months of each other. Actually, it's the quadruple whammy because my wife likes to celebrate our meet-a-versary. Actually, it is the quintuple whammy because my wife likes to celebrate our kiss-a-versary. Which means within the space of just a few weeks, I'm on the hook for some of her biggest celebratory expectations. It's a gift gauntlet, I tell ya.

I love my wife, so I am thrilled to celebrate all of these, but I get stressed about gifts for each of them, and figuring out if gifts are expected for all of them.

I believe that Christmas should absolutely be a gift holiday, and of course, the birthday should be a gift day as well. Valentine's Day should be something thoughtful (curse those inflated, overpriced Valentine's Day flowers), and meet-a-versary and kiss-a-versary are just something that we should spend some nice time together.

I think the biggest problem of all is Valentine's Day. There is this pressure from society to get flowers, a card, chocolates, a gift, and an expensive dinner. I mean, we're talking about hundreds of dollars if you add all that up, not counting the babysitter. How is a man supposed to survive that holiday?

You don't want to get me started on "Sweetest Day," which is a holiday that certain parts of the country celebrate in October. (Deep breaths, okay, focus, Tommy.)

My wife is everything to me, but wouldn't it be okay to show that in a thoughtful gift, a romantic note, and a nice dinner, and ditch all the other commercialized trappings?

If we don't draw the line somewhere, I'm afraid that we're going to have to sell our house, because we've spent all of our money giving each other and our kids gifts every month.

I realize that I may be on the unpopular side of this topic, but this is all coming from a man that doesn't need any gifts. I just want to feel loved and appreciated, and have a wonderful time with my wife on each one of these holidays.

PS I love you, my bride.

For the most part, I've taken all the pressure off Tommy having to buy any gifts. I take care of the gifts for the kids. The only gifts he needs to buy are the ones for me, and I've tried to simplify that as much as possible. A few years back, I made a deal with him. Since coming up with a gift idea four times a year caused him so much stress, I suggested a particular item that he could gift me over and over so that he would never have to think of what to get me again.

Reassuring him, I said, "Just book me a spa day."

That would ensure three to four spa days a year for me to relish in. Moms rarely prioritize self-care, so this gift strategy perfectly carves out a seasonal getaway to the local spa, most often while the kids are in school. I check in early to take advantage of all the amenities before my massage or facial. This chance for me to step away and reset is absolutely glorious. And you know what else? I am a better mom because of it.

Remember, Mamas, self-love and self-care are not selfish!

And since my husband does not come from the "love of pampering" camp, I explained the appeal of the spa in a way he would understand…"Babe, spa days are like _____ for a guy; it never gets old."

You can fill in the blank since a lady never tells. ☺

Alright, ladies and gentlemen, it's time for you to choose whose side you are on!

From the mom corner...Gifts are a language of their own, and it's okay to speak on ALL the special days.

From the dad corner...Making sure your family feels loved and appreciated on meaningful holidays is important, but it's also important to be careful about overspending. Saving for your family's future is its own kind of celebration. And then there's this: Kids should know that life is about heartfelt experiences, not stuff.

Whose side are you on...MOM or DAD?

The Co-Sleeping vs. Sleep Training Debate

For the longest time, I would say, "Heck no!" to having more humanity in my sleeping quarters with me in addition to my wife. I understand the upside of kids in your bed. They are supercute, their childhood is going to fly by (I know it is for our kids), and they are just awesome.

HOWEVER, I felt like it really affected the relationship I had with my wife. There are many times when I used to just head to the couch when I knew one of our little ones was going to be in our bed. Reason being, around the age of three, our daughter turned into quite the kicker at night. Kicking me in the face, the gut, everywhere. While she was sleeping, she would just start kicking.

Okay, so hear me out. Every single morning, I wake up to these eight words whispered in my ear…

"I love you just the way you are."

Who says this every morning? My baby girl. Not my husband.

My baby.

She is four. She is my last. She is my rainbow baby. She came after one of the most difficult times in my life. She is my living, breathing reminder to have hope. She is feisty and sleeps restlessly like her mom. She is immediately settled if she has any type of skin-to-skin contact with me, not excluding foot to face, which happens a lot. It probably has to do with the fact that when I delivered her, she didn't leave my chest for hours and hours. I wouldn't let her go.

Listen, sometimes I want to get intimate with my wife! What is so wrong with that? Well, if there is a kid that wants to sleep in your bed, this may not be possible. I might have to spend twenty minutes trying to get my kiddo to sleep in the other room just so I can sleep with her mom!

Each night, all of my kids actually start out in their own beds. But somewhere in the middle of the night, my littlest finds her way into bed with us. In my opinion, this is the best of both worlds; my husband has me at bedtime for "the sex" if the occasion "arises," and I still get to cuddle and hug my baby for a good portion of the later night and early morning. One of my favorite parts of the day consists of those predawn early morning cuddles and then when the two older ones crawl into bed with me a little later. Tommy is up at 4:00 a.m. every day, so what difference does it make to him what we do? But he is so strongly against it.

Sometimes that timing doesn't quite work out. If we're getting back from a date night, the pressure might be on to "make out right away before the kids wake up." I can remember specifically because it happened just last week. I seduced my wife to join me in the bedroom around midnight, and then our four-year-old started crying for us right at midnight-oh-one. Long story short, it took about an hour to get her back to sleep, before my wife and I could "connect." Was it worth the wait? Absolutely! Do I wish I didn't have to work that hard to get some time alone with my wife? Absolutely!

If someone asked what is the number one topic Tommy and I fight over it would be sleep. Ever since our first child was born, we had different takes on how our littles should sleep. Tommy was and still is hard-core into the sleep-training method.

This is very true, we argued about it from the very beginning. Everything I read about sleep training was that it will be terrible, but that it would make your life so much better once you do it. And it was true! It totally worked when we stuck to it. Suddenly, my wife and I had our lives back after 6:00 or 7:00 p.m. We had a good thing going on for a bunch of years, until we took our youngest out of her crib way too early.

If you listen to only one piece of parenting advice from this book, let it be this. Keep your kid in a crib as long as possible. Get a net to keep them from climbing out of the crib if you need to. Ever since our youngest daughter (who WAS an amazing sleeper in her crib days) moved into a "big-girl bed" before her second birthday, nights have been pure chaos.

While consistency is paramount for children, I always allowed wiggle room when it came to kids and sleep. For example, if my kids didn't feel good or if they had a bad dream, I always wanted them to know Mom and Dad were just down the hall. But I always seemed to cave a bit to my husband when I was a sleep-deprived postpartum mom nursing all hours of the night and desperately wanted to sleep. Sleep training meant our kiddos would sleep for six plus hours at a time, and that all sounded heavenly until I had to endure earth-shattering cries coming from the nursery. It went against everything in my fiber. Tommy would send me out at night so I wouldn't hear the crying and so that he could sleep train the baby. We would then settle into a nice habit, but once the baby got sick or was teething, we were back to square one. I think we re–sleep trained our oldest until she was five years old.

A little backstory. Being the youngest of twelve kids, I can neither confirm nor deny that I slept with my parents well into my elementary-school-age years. Part of it had to do with me being a bed wetter, so after I peed my bed, I'd crawl into bed next to my mom. But I was her baby, so she allowed it. (I also learned to do my own laundry at a super-young age because of it.)

Ironic that the man who thinks allowing our kids to sleep with us will do long-term, permanent damage to our kids ended up marrying a bed wetter who slept with her parents until fourth grade...hey, you picked me, buddy!

One of my biggest issues with the lack of a sleep schedule is that it has affected other people too. Every now and then my wife and I like to take a little vacation as a couple, and my parents have been so gracious to watch our kids. Well, as these mini getaways approach, we have to retrain our daughter to sleep in her bed, because we don't want her waking up my parents in the middle of the night. This can lead to a stressful pre-vacation week for all of us just trying to get our little girl to sleep like a big girl as our departure date approaches.

In the end, this was a topic that we could never agree on, and I didn't see my wife's mom instincts ever changing, so I realized I need to look at the positive in it. Now that most of our four-year-old's "kicking and screaming in the middle of the night" phase is over, it is pretty nice to wake up in the morning and look at her innocent face.

As long as she falls asleep in her bed (which she does) so I can spend some time with just my wife in our bed, I'm okay with our last baby jumping in our bed in the middle of the night. But not through her elementary school years (ahem).

Alright, ladies and gentlemen, it's time for you to choose whose side you are on!

From the mom corner...Let 'em in! It's not gonna last forever.

From the dad corner...Each person has their own bed, and that is where they should sleep! You married your spouse so you could sleep together forever in a bed, alone. Vote for this side so this author can get his wife back again at night!

Whose side are you on...MOM or DAD?

Should You Stress About the Mess?

Let me start by saying if Marie Kondo or HGTV is looking for their next hot mess household, look no further!

Our house is messy, y'all. Like really really messy. I don't mean in a theoretical way. I don't mean that I have some drawers that are jumbled and some closets that are bursting. I mean seriously messy. Reportedly messy. Reality TV kind of messy.

It's so messy that I once walked over ten thousand steps in one day (per my Fitbit) just putting things away and cleaning my house.

It's so messy that I have legit fears of my cleaning lady walking in one day and quitting.

Over the past decade, we have collected so much stuff and crap that consumes every nook and cranny of our place. It is probably the biggest stressor currently in my life, by far. I start out on a mission to get things organized, and it ultimately is just me restacking piles and putting those piles in new places. And you know what doesn't help? My husband and kids don't seem to see it or care about the mess. They are far more bothered by the insane mad lady I become because of it.

OMG, just writing about this raises my heart rate and blood

pressure. And I don't foresee a solution anytime soon, which makes me want to cry. Actually, I'm gonna need a minute.

Wait wait wait wait...let's talk about all this stuff and crap that we have. Where did it all come from? Overpriced souvenirs and way too many gifts perhaps (refer to the appropriate chapters). The solution is simple: Stop buying the stuff!

Since this is a self-inflicted wound as I see it, I don't stress about the mess. We have three kids and two dogs. Our home is going to be messy for the foreseeable future. Should we all work a little bit harder on keeping it clean? For sure. Should we stress? Heck no!

I have tried going the kids' chores route. Incentives for cleaning up. Taking a garbage bag out, threatening to toss everything on the floor. But admittedly, Tommy and I stink at follow-through. Some days I'm stronger than others, staying consistent. But other days, the whining and crying that proceeds for hours on end because they don't want to clean sends me into mental exhaustion.

Plain and simple, it's our own fault because we don't hold the kids accountable.

I agree, it's on both of us.

So instead, we live like animals, our house looks like a tornado hit it on a daily basis, and no one seems to care except me. I have legit spent hours and hours, sometimes eight to nine hours a day, cleaning up, only to have it destroyed in eight to nine minutes. It is so defeating!

And because of this, I live each day in complete horror, worried a friend or family member will show up unexpectedly.

I'm not living in horror of visitors seeing the mess. We have gotten exactly what we asked for. We had a large family, and now we have a messy home.

I do agree with Lucy that it is time to get the kids on board and make house cleaning a team sport.

I would say that time should have been when they were toddlers. They would have gotten accustomed to cleaning up at an early age. Now, they are older and more resistant. Again, our fault.

As I write this, our kids are ten, eight, and five. The older ones should certainly be doing chores, and the five-year-old would totally be down, as she seems to like structure the most out of all of them! We can still inject chores into our family routine, to combat our kids' raging case of choreitis.

There is zero excuse for our kids not helping out around the house, especially when I think about the ages I was as a kid when I helped out with chores.

At ten years old, I was making my own breakfasts and school lunches.

At eight years old, I knew how to do my own laundry. (When you are a bed wetter, you learn to do laundry at a young age.)

At five years old, whatever toys I possessed (which was not a lot) would disappear if I did not pick up after myself.

I'm sure we need to set up some sort of incentive system so they get their chores done, right? I know, this is not a proud parent moment, I'm trying to figure this out as I'm writing it. Alright, I'm gonna try to implement a chore plan this weekend. Done deal.

One kid can be in charge of sweeping.

One kid can be in charge of carrying two bags around the house, one for garbage, and one for items that need to be moved to other parts of the house.

One kid can be in charge of loading plates into the dishwasher.

You've gotta start somewhere, right? And I think after I see how that works, I'll get back to you...

In the meantime. I'm not gonna stress.

Moral of the story, learn from us and give your kids age-appropriate chores and hold them accountable. Otherwise, you'll end up stressed out like me!!

HGTV, call me.

Alright, ladies and gentlemen, it's time for you to choose whose side you are on!

From the mom corner…Stress Mess is a real condition. Figuring out how to deal with the mess leads to more stress. Clean is the only thing that stops Stress Mess. Right?

From the dad corner…Let's just relax a bit. As long as the kids are young, the house is gonna be messy. It's gonna get cleaner someday. (Right?) Until then, embrace the chaos.

Whose side are you on…MOM or DAD?

How Much Should You Pay a Babysitter?

A good babysitter is so important! They are watching and caring for the most precious thing for parents...our kids.

With that said, should the rate we pay babysitters change based on their experience and whether the kids are sleeping? Absolutely, I say!

We've had a few great babysitters and we love them. Our three kids and two dogs can be a handful, so they deserve every bit of the fifteen dollars per hour we pay them.

However, some of our sitters get off easy. They just watch TV with the kiddos and feed them popcorn. I have a few things I'd like to propose.

Flat rates should be allowed for anything over four hours. You shouldn't have to keep tacking on fifteen dollars per hour at that point. Kind of like parking, maybe there is an hourly fee for the first three, and then a flat rate after that? I get so nervous when the babysitter meter is running when my wife and I are out to dinner. The dollar total just keeps ramping up in my mind, the same mind that is supposed to be paying full attention to my wife. Do I really want to see that movie if it is going to cost us one hundred dollars? Once we've bought two tickets and a bucket of popcorn, we've already hit the fifty-dollar mark, and then when you tack on the three more hours needed for the movie and driving home, that's an additional fifty dollars for the baby-sitter. What movies are worth paying one hundred dollars to see in a theater?

And it seems reasonable to me that the hours after the kids fall asleep should remain productive on the part of the babysitter, instead of an invitation to sit down and watch our Netflix account. What about helping pick up after the kids? A little bit of light cleaning? Running the washing machine? Look, if I were paying someone to come work on my yard or to help with some administrative work, I'd want them working the whole time, not sitting on my couch Instagramming away.

First of all, Tommy, if your goal is for us to never be able to book a babysitter again, then bravo, you did it. After this book comes out, our family will be put on some babysitter blacklist.

Secondly, if any of our babysitters (past or present) are currently reading this right now, I just want to say, "I love you. I appreciate you. Don't ever change. Tommy knows not what he says."

Now that we've gotten that out of the way, here is my take.

You've probably heard the saying "Everyone should work in a restaurant at least once in their life." There is a reason this quote is wildly popular and true. Servers, bussers, cooks, and hosts deal with a lot, and part of what they have to deal with most notably is some of the lowest levels of human behavior when it comes to impatient, fussy, or downright mean customers. By working in a restaurant, you gain a tremendous perspective, understanding, and compassion for what restaurant staff go through. I was a hostess for many years in my early twenties. The fancier the restaurant, the worse the humans tended to be toward the waitstaff. I will never forget the time I was working as a hostess at the Grand Luxe Cafe in LA, and a woman yelled at me because I attempted to hang up her coat on the coatrack after she draped it over another booth, where a family was seated. She scolded, "This coat costs more than your life." At the time, I was young and I allowed those words to cut me down. Now, I use those words as a reminder to always try my best to treat workers, no matter the rank and level, with dignity and respect. So when it comes to the babysitters we bring into our home, I've worked that restaurant, so to speak.

Speaking of respect, I absolutely love and respect these lovely young ladies who come over and babysit my babies. Most of them are in high school and college, so every four years or so I see them go off and do great things. Some will bring over their book bags on a weekend night to study while the kids sleep so that Tommy and I can have a much-needed night out. And to me, that is priceless time to nurture our marriage, no "babysitter calculator" needed here. My kids get so excited when one of our babysitters comes over. They paint nails, braid hair, draw, play, read, and sing until my littles are in a deep slumber. So what if they watch TV?!

They just successfully put all of our kids to bed, which is no easy feat, let me tell you!

I think I got my first babysitting job at twelve years old and continued to babysit well into my midtwenties. Even while I was working as a hostess, I babysat for local families. Living in LA is not cheap, so I worked several jobs to make ends meet. For decades, I was blessed to mostly have wonderful families to work for that treated me as one of their own. And now that the roles are reversed and I'm the parent hiring sitters, it is so important to me that our babysitters feel valued and appreciated for the loving care they provide to my kids.

No, I don't think they should be paid less even if the kids are sleeping.

No, I don't expect them to clean my house. I do expect it to look the way I left it though. (Which, as we covered in a previous chapter, means somewhere between a dumpster fire and an episode of *Hoarders*.)

No, I don't think there should be a flat rate; you wouldn't want your hourly job to lowball you.

PS Tommy means well, I know he does. He's just never relied on babysitting to pay the bills. I have. So, I got you, babysitters, please don't blacklist us.

Alright, ladies and gentlemen, it's time for you to choose whose side you are on!

From the mom corner…Babysitters should be babysitting, not doing housekeeping, not working multiple hours for a flat rate. And it's important to not get blacklisted by the babysitters' union.

From the dad corner…Babysitters should function like any other contractor we would bring into our home, with a list of things to be accomplished while we're gone. It's the real world, and watching TV doesn't qualify as something that I want to pay someone fifteen dollars an hour for.

Whose side are you on…MOM or DAD?

Should You Cut Your Kids' Hair or Take Them to the Salon?

My parents cut my hair in my younger years, and I ended up with quite a few bowl cuts.

However, I think from the age of about twelve, I started going to the barbershop with my dad to get my hair cut. I've been having my hair cut for many years now, and know all the important steps when cutting a boy's hair.

1. Choose a number for the clippers on the sides and back.
2. Use scissors on the top.
3. Use a combination of longer clippers and scissors to blend the two.

That, my friends, is the perfect haircut for boys. And I know how to do it.

I've been the chief trimmer for our eight-year-old son for most of his life. It's a bonding experience, and I love it.

Few things make me prouder than seeing a nice haircut I have given my son, and I must admit that I've gotten pretty good at it. Some might just call me a barber. Or, actually, since we live in Los Angeles, "stylist" might be the term of preference.

I'm not brave enough to suggest to my wife that I can cut her hair, or our oldest daughter's either. I will say, I could do our youngest daughter's hair. She's four, and she just has straight hair. So I could get a pair of scissors and cut the bottom. No problem at all. Our older daughter has graduated to a bob hairstyle, which I'm not skilled enough to tackle. I'm not messing with that. My wife has some cool-looking bangs, so I'm not going to try to trim her hair either. I understand my limits; I have chosen my muse. My son's hair, and possibly my youngest daughter's hair, those I can do.

Personally, I've been going to Supercuts for years now. I've looked for good barbershops in LA, but haven't been really able to find the right one. So, Supercuts it is. Call it a salon, call it whatever you want. I tell them to use a number four razor on the sides and back and to trim it up top. Then blend. It's that same formula I use when I cut my son's hair, except that I wear my hair spiky and my son likes to comb his hair with a part.

My problem with salons is twofold.

1. They are expensive.
2. They are often not as knowledgeable about men's hair as me.

Okay, actually threefold.

3. Sometimes the beauticians get so caught up in conversation that they don't do the best job at cutting hair. Stay

focused on the job. We don't need to be close friends; I just
want a good haircut.

Now, I get it. I understand why they want to talk...they're bored.
They've been cutting hair all day long!

I've gotten bad haircuts from salons way too many times to
remember, so I've decided to take the skills I've learned and put them
to use, giving my son the best haircut he could imagine (and saving
twenty-seven dollars).

There's probably one thing I should mention here...my son HATES
when I cut his hair. It's not because he thinks I don't do a good job;
he just hates the process of it. He'd much rather go out and have it
professionally done, and he lets me hear it.

So, this bonding experience with my son may not be mutually
appreciated. And he's getting a bit older now, so who knows what our
next couple of years of haircuts will bring.

Last spring, I had to bribe my son to start practicing baseball.
Baseball was another father-son bond he wasn't quite into. Why is this
relevant, and how did I bribe him? Well, I told him if he would start
practicing baseball with me each night, I would start taking him to a
salon to get his hair trimmed. The father-son haircut bond would be
replaced by a father-son baseball bond. He was all in!

But now that baseball season is over, it's time to start cutting hair
again.

Three days. Three days is the length of time that one of Tommy's
haircuts looks good on our son before he starts to resemble the next
client on *Botched*. The hairs start to grow out in all different directions,

and as much water as I use, I just can't quite get those Alfalfa strays down. Not by coincidence, this never happens after our boy gets his hair professionally trimmed.

Now I am by no means claiming to know how to cut hair. I once did it to my two-year-old after just giving birth to her younger brother.

In general, it's probably never a good idea to make any rash decisions while sleep deprived with a newborn and a toddler. Yet there I was, thinking my two-year-old would look cute with bangs. The result? My sweet baby girl resembled the likes of Mommy and Daddy's eighties bowl haircuts…in 2012. It was baaaaaaad.

I vowed never again. I have retired any scissors, promising to never attempt to cut my kid's hair again. And I hope that Tommy will follow my lead and hang up his!

Alright, ladies and gentlemen, it's time for you to choose whose side you are on!

From the mom corner…For just a few dollars, a trained professional will evenly and expertly trim, style, and groom your child, no muss, no fuss. Worth it? Abso-freaking-lutely.

From the dad corner…If you've got the skills, use 'em. Trim those straggly ends, take the trimmer to those shaggy sides. It saves a few bucks and creates bonding. At the very least, skip the salon and hit Supercuts.

Whose side are you on…MOM or DAD?

Should You Take Your Kids to Restaurants?

Listen, there are families that we have seen at restaurants where the parents and young kids seem so happy. The entire family is laughing, trying new foods, and overall having a really pleasant time.

And if you are one of those families, congratulations! You have won at parenthood.

Well, my friends, that is not our family. I'm sure this will change as the kids get older, but for the first ten years of parenting, going to a restaurant has been extremely stressful. As in wildly stressful. As in, a colonoscopy sounds like more fun than being trapped in a restaurant booth with my kids.

First off, our kids don't try new foods. Is that our fault as parents? Probably. And I'm sure it doesn't help that my wife and I are picky eaters as well. Italian food is about as ethnic as we get. But we are what we are, so deal with it! But when I say that the kids don't try new foods, they don't even want to try familiar foods presented in a different way than what they are used to. Mac and cheese has to look like the kind we make at home, or it's a nonstarter. And anything out of a usual cuisine category for them is an absolute no.

Second, our kids' behavior at restaurants always escalates. They have no patience for the food-ordering process and start asking for their food right away. Before we have even ordered. The asking turns to whining, the whining turns to wiggling wildly in their seats, the wiggling turns into crying.

Because the only thing they are exposed to on a regular basis is fast food, which is immediate.

Third, when they are hungry, they tend to start getting on each other's nerves rather quickly, and then they start fighting with or picking on each other. My son Tommy "accidentally" elbows his younger sister Katie. She squeals. Big sister Babs clamps her hands over her ears and loudly proclaims how annoying they both are. Katie wails that Babs is making fun of her, and brother Tommy starts to toss shards of shredded napkin into big sister Babs's drink, which sets her off on a new tangent. Oh, the fun!

You could say the same about us when we are out on a date and hungry at restaurants. We start fighting and picking on each other… until the bread basket arrives. It's called hangry, that state of thinking you're irritated, but really, you're just famished.

This leads to a super-stressed mom and dad during the meal. Personally, I'm thinking about how much money we're spending on having a bad time, while my wife is often worried about what the other diners in the restaurant think of our wild table.

I've just had a potential moment of revelation. What if we are the reason for all of this? Before even sitting down, we are expecting our kids to be wild, which immediately stresses us out. Kids pick up on their parents' emotions, which results in everyone stressing out. Not to get too California esoteric, but maybe we're manifesting this meal mayhem.

I do have some solutions for all of the above issues, but it is all so much work, I'd just rather stay home.

On occasion, I've experienced some success when I've taken just one of my kids out to a restaurant. Maybe it's a mommy-daughter brunch or a mother-son dinner date. Regardless, they are a million times better behaved when their siblings aren't around.

When we do end up going to a restaurant, I'll actually *bring* food for the kids. That's right, I pack food so we can go out to eat. This is so they have something to snack on while we wait for their meal (Cheerios and Goldfish work well), which buys us some time and saves us from buying an extra appetizer that my kids wouldn't eat.

But by the time the entrees arrive, the kids are so hopped up on snacks that they don't even eat the meal. And then you're stressed about paying for food they don't eat…but you literally did this to yourself by packing snacks!

When their behavior escalates, we're basically trying to do anything to calm them down. Usually for me that is taking our youngest and leaving the table, walking around the restaurant for a while. So yeah, when we go out to eat, I often don't have the chance to sit down all that much.

When the kids start fighting with each other, we'll end up threatening them with taking away privileges. It turns the dinner table into a conference table, with negotiations and debates. Oh, the good times!

After we all finish up our entire stressful meal, my wife often feels bad for the servers, and then we leave an extra tip for the craziness and mess that our family caused.

It's standard restaurant protocol. The bigger the mess, the more you tip. Same goes for hotel rooms. By default, kids tend to leave bigger messes, so you need to tip more for all the smashed-up Cheerios and Goldfish you brought from home. Call it a Cheerios and Goldfish tax.

In the end, going to a restaurant is a stressful time that just costs us a whole lot of money, when we could have just eaten at home. Oh, parenthood!

But we've got to do it. We've got to take our wild kids out into the wilds of dining. How are kids supposed to know how to act in public places like a restaurant if parents never take them there?!

A lot of the above is our own fault.

Picky eaters? Our fault.

Won't eat the food after eating snacks? Our fault.

You know who are really good at restaurants? Kids who are only children. I'm also convinced that whoever came up with the bright idea to have school "restaurant nights" must have only one kid because those events are next-level chaos. School restaurant nights are fundraisers where all the families in your kid's class go to a designated restaurant together. The scene is bananas, with kids running and shrieking times a hundred. And you can see my only-child theory tested out in real time on school restaurant nights. The kids from single-child families are sitting calmly beside their parental units just cool as cucumbers. Meanwhile, all the other kids and their siblings look like a junior version of some spring break special on MTV.

Our kids? Their wild behavior feeds off each other until it is an endless series of *Kids Behaving Badly*. And like every bad reality TV show, viewers watch in horror, some disgusted while others are highly entertained because their lives now look so much better than the nightmare happening at our table.

But....

This won't change unless we keep gathering our courage and taking our kids out. It may take some serious time, it's for sure going to take varsity levels of patience. But I am doubling down here and say not only should we take our kids to restaurants, we should plan to take them on a weekly basis!

Huh? Who can afford taking a family of five to a restaurant on a weekly basis?

Going out to eat at a restaurant is a privilege. Throughout my childhood, my parents took us out to eat only on very special occasions. And I remember those occasions as being really special!

I remember a trip to Macaroni Grill after graduation. I remember my parents taking my older sister out to El Torito for her sixteenth birthday.

Honestly, most of our memories were made at home (or on camping trips), and that was all we knew. My sisters and I turned out just fine not really going to restaurants when we were under the age of fifteen.

I'm gonna go fire up the Crock-Pot now, because that is what family eating is really about.

Alright, ladies and gentlemen, it's time for you to choose whose side you are on!

From the mom corner…Yes, it's a pain. Yes, the kids act terribly. Yes, it is crazy-town stressful. But it's important to take the kids out to eat so that over time, they will get better at it. We've got to keep our eye on the goal of eventually having a somewhat reasonable, generally well-mannered eating-out experience…with our children there.

From the dad corner…Taking the kids out to eat is expensive, stressful, and not enjoyable! Maybe it's something to try again in a few years. But for now, we're better off staying home with the toaster oven!

Whose side are you on…MOM or DAD?

When Is the Right Time to Talk to Your Kids About Sex?

As a father, there are few defining moments I think I should absolutely be a part of; teaching our kids to ride a bike, the birds and the bees chat with my son...you know, the big ones.

I taught my son how to ride a bike. Check! I taught him how to play baseball. Check! I taught him how to tie his shoes. Check! I taught him that the Patriots are the greatest NFL team. Check!

When my son was seven, I just assumed I still had a bit of time until the discussion explaining sex to him. To be honest, my wife and I never talked about when we would have it, but I thought that it was my thing. In all the movies, dads have that talk with their sons.

Well, one day my son asked me, "Dad, if I go on vacation with any girl and if I lay in bed with her, will she then become pregnant?"

Wait, what? I took a deep breath. Reminder, my son was seven at the time. "Son, did somebody at school tell you this?"

"No, Mama did." Wait, what?

While I was still processing the first question, the second one came. "Dad, what if you don't want your penis to make a girl pregnant?"

Wait, what?

I was stunned and didn't react, so I kind of froze up. My son was having the birds and the bees chat with me instead of me having it with him. I did my best to answer his questions while remaining literally dumbfounded as to why my wife would have talked to him about all of this. It was my job to have the sex talk with my son. I always assumed Lucy would do this with our daughters, while I assumed she assumed I'd have the chat with my son. Maybe I'm guilty of assuming too much while not communicating enough...

Once I had some time to gather myself after wrapping up this unexpected convo with my seven-year-old, I went and talked to my wife. She admitted that the day before on a car ride, she had had this convo with our other two kids in the car as well. Wait, what? Our nine-year-old and three-year-old girls also heard all of this info?

I let my wife know that I was bummed we hadn't discussed this first. This is one of those parenting moments that I wanted to be in charge of. I felt like it was my job to have the sex talk with my son, and now it had already been done. And we only have one son.

I was over it a few minutes later, but for real, shouldn't we have discussed first? I think big moments in a kid's childhood, when possible, should be communicated better between the parents.

So, a little backstory.

As you know, I grew up in a super-Catholic family, hence the twelve kids. Sex and any act within the realm of sex was not discussed or talked about. Catholic school also did not do much for the curious kids when it came to sex. They touched on the basic puberty topics but it's not like we had this in-depth Q&A. Back in the 1980s and '90s, the nuns would never allow it. In my house, you were told you don't have sex or speak of it until after marriage. Mind you, several of my nieces and nephews are a result of this method of parental noncommunication. Don't get me wrong, I love my parents more than life; they are two of the greatest parents any kid would be lucky to have. I also love my faith deeply and love the fact that I went to Catholic school. But the birds and the bees chat? Not exactly their strong suit.

Talking about sex was taboo. But here's the thing about kids; they are curious breeds that will seek out answers wherever they can find them. For me, I learned a bit from MTV's *The Grind*. For those of you who aren't familiar with this program, it was this big dance party that would feature young adults dancing and grinding on each other, oftentimes with merely a bathing suit layer between each other's private parts. It was quite scandalous, especially the spring break editions. Piecing together scenes from *The Grind* and a few static-filled R-rated cable channels combined with what the kids in the neighborhood would share was my version of the birds and the bees talk. I had a lot of questions that I wanted to ask but was just too embarrassed. I thought babies came out of belly buttons far later in life than I'd like to admit. There was no Google or YouTube to search.

I knew I wanted to take a different approach when I became a parent.

So, from day one, I would talk openly to my kids about their private parts, calling them the proper anatomical name, penis, vagina, breasts, and so forth. There was never a defining moment where I started these talks; it was just a continuation of an open dialogue about body parts, what was to be kept private and the function of each part. For example, instead of telling my older two kids, three and five years old at the time, that their baby sister came out of Mommy's belly, I would say she came out of my vagina. (I would place money on it that Tommy is sweating and already embarrassed of the way I'm talking.) I would let my kids watch me breastfeed, explaining how they all drank milk from Mommy's breasts when they were babies.

And one day while driving in the car, my son was confused about how each of them were made up of half Mommy and half Daddy. "But, Mommy, how is Katie part Daddy if you carried her in your belly?" I think that's a fair question. So, I explained in a very matter-of-fact-way how the sperm from Daddy's penis went inside Mommy's vagina and found one of Mommy's eggs and that process would fertilize into a baby. By no means do I think this constitutes the birds and the bees talk. It's just my continuation of having an open dialogue about our body parts.

This is where I think our difference really shows up. See, to me, any discussion about sex is the birds and the bees talk. I get that Lucy sees the definition of "the talk" as a more formal sit-down kind of situation. But I also know that these topics are going to come up at the craziest times, while at the grocery store, while listening to a song...you can't always schedule when it could come up. In my mind, hearing what they discussed in the car that day, the bird and the bees talk is already done. Now, when the time is right, I'll certainly have another chat with him coming from Dad's point of view, but he already has all of the details! He's learned all of the most important info already.

Yeah, I just have a very different idea of simply answering questions as they come up versus a true "coming-of-age," "first-steps-to-manhood" kind of a thing. You might be feeling sorry for Tommy, robbed of his chance to bond with his son. But I promise you, it's been a natural process, this growing awareness for the kids and the questions that understandably follow. I guess the questions Tommy and I need to answer between each other are what constitutes a "birds and the bees–level" talk, and what is open season when it comes to the open forum of discussion and questions from the kids.

In my mind, there has been no official sit-down birds and the bees talk with any one of our kids. Have there been questions? Sure. Have I answered them? Yes. But I feel like there is still so much more for them to know. And when that happens, I absolutely plan to involve both parents. I may have Tom step out halfway through the girls' talks, but I believe that is normal, and I would be fine with Tommy spearheading our son's, as long as the information is literal and truthful so our kids know what's up.

Lastly, this is the main, and most important, reason for my approach, and my apologies for going too dark on this topic...

Statistics show that one in three girls are sexually abused during their childhood before the age of eighteen. In boys, it is one in five. This is terrifying to read as a parent. I personally know far too many loved ones in my life that were sexually abused as a child or minor. Experts agree that one of the primary ways to prevent such horrific behavior is to have an open dialogue with your children about being the boss of their bodies, not being afraid to speak up and set boundaries, knowing what are defined as private parts, and being able to differentiate between these parts. It is paramount that my children feel safe and comfortable asking their parents anything, knowing we will always listen and believe them.

With all of this said, I would like to point out how much I love my husband and respect him so much as a father. I love that this topic means so much to him. I love that he wants to play an active role in important discussions like sex with our son. One of the many reasons I fell in love with this man was his incredible belief in the good of humanity. His parents raised him in a super-safe environment, protected from much of the evil in the world. It's only natural that he wants to raise his own children in a similar way. Nothing means more to us in this world than keeping our children safe, happy, and healthy. Everything we do stems from that same goal. And because of that, I take comfort in knowing we will find the right balance when it comes to the birds and the bees talk.

We debated whether or not to even put it in the book since it carries such a serious tone…But I just refuse to let my kids learn about sex from MTV.

I just wanted to jump back in and say I think the way that Lucy is comfortable having such detailed talks with our kids is wonderful. I understand her reasoning, and fully support her being so open with the kids. And I agree, the most important thing is keeping children safe, happy, and healthy. I really appreciate Lucy's clarity on that message. Since we have different takes on how pretty much everything is done, there will always be more communicating we need to do, and I'm fully open to figuring that out because I love my wife and family so much.

Alright, ladies and gentlemen, it's time for you to choose whose side you are on!

From the mom corner…Answer any questions that come up, whenever and wherever they are asked. Make conversation about sex an ongoing one, not a onetime "birds and the bees" event.

From the dad corner…Dads should have the sex talk with their sons. The next time this conversation comes up between Mom and our little man, the topic should be tabled so Dad can be involved in the discussion as well.

Whose side are you on…MOM or DAD?

What about you? Is one of you more comfortable talking about sex and body parts? Is it more difficult for one of you? And here's an important question: Why? What do you think is the right age to have "the talk" with your kids? And what does "the talk" mean to each of you? Should information about sex and the body be the realm of a particular parent based on gender, or should it be based on who has a greater level of comfort talking about it?

At What Age Should You Get Your Kids a Cell Phone?

I can't even with this topic. I got my first cell phone when I graduated from college. Yep, I was twenty-one years old, and my parents got me a cell as a graduation gift.

I had studied hard for seventeen years straight, and then I earned my first cell phone. Thanks, Mom and Dad, for keeping me focused on my education and not distracted by gadgets.

That was in 2001.

I fully understand that times have changed. Here we are, two decades later, and as I write this, I have a ten-year-old, an eight-year-old, and a four-year-old.

These kiddos are much more sophisticated on my and Lucy's iPhones than I wish, but I can proudly say that not one of them has ever asked for their own phone. So, at this point, it's not even a conversation point for us.

They are still at the age that we pick them up from school every day, and we know exactly where they are at all times. So I'm thinking, maybe the second or third year of high school is when they might get their first phone. And I'm thinking that a pretty straightforward old-school flip phone will be the way to go when that day comes.

When they are somewhere and they need to get in contact with us, that would be cell phone time. I remember when I was in high school, my parents and I had a pay phone trick. In order to not waste a quarter, I would call home and hang up after one ring. Then I would call home again, and hang up after one ring. When you hang up a call from a pay phone before the person on the other end answers, you get your quarter back! When the phone rang just once two times in a row, my parents then knew it was time to come and pick me up. Yep, now maybe you know where my frugalness comes from.

Today, our cell phones' area code is different than our city's, so I'm not certain the quarter trick would work, and I'm pretty sure they don't have pay phones at high schools anymore, right? Come to think of it, I don't think I've seen a pay phone anywhere in quite a while.

So yeah, I'm thinking at some point in high school it will be time to get our kids phones. But that DOES NOT mean they will be getting the latest iPhone. The phones they receive will be for phone calls and texting only, no apps or social media.

Of course, cell phones have their uses, and I do see how, at the right age, a cell phone could be an important part of how our kids stay in touch with us, a safety item that will make Lucy and me rest easier as our teenagers begin the process of becoming more and more independent. But when I think about the cost associated with cell phones, when I read about kids getting addicted to their phones and all the apps, when I hear about the hours and hours kids are spending on social media and the way that social media can compromise a kid's self-esteem, it's hard for me to see any value in putting a phone into the hands of my kids before it's necessary or before they're ready. And then there's the fact that Lucy and I have enough phones to keep up with right now. I can only imagine the extra crazy if we were trying to find our kids' lost cell phones and chargers in addition to ours!

If my wife can present some solutions to those concerns, then we can start actually talking about a cell phone in a few years, but not yet!

Our oldest has in fact started asking for a phone, contrary to my husband's selective hearing on this matter. I'm pretty sure Tommy is living in denial about the fact that our oldest is on the brink of preteen territory. But I also think my oldest wanting a phone is actually fueled by our middle child, who is very eager to get a phone of his own. And since he knows these gifts go in birth order, he's actively nudging her along. She could honestly wait until she is sixteen, but my middle is ready to have his phone yesterday. So, the two of them settled on ten years old as a fair age to receive a phone. Not that Tommy and I were consulted about this protocol.

It was just November of 2019 when our family purchased our very first iPad. That's right, I made it nine years with three kids without an iPad before biting that "Apple." And I'm not gonna lie, the convenience of my kid having a phone or a tablet is most definitely appealing. There are the obvious reasons, like having a moment of calm and quiet in the house, but a device also helps when the kids are at a friend's house and need to communicate with you, or if something happens at school or while you are traveling for work. As a mom, I have a magnetic pull to be close to my kids; I like the idea of my children having direct access to me and me to them. I'd like to think it's a tool for them to know their mama is only a phone call away.

Like Tommy, I was also twenty-one years old, a junior in college, when I got my first phone. But it wasn't because my parents wanted me to wait until I was that age. That's just when cell phones were becoming more mainstream. And if Tommy is being real, there is no way he would have waited until he was twenty-one to get a phone if he were being raised now. Cell phones are so mainstream today; I think kids should have them based on their family dynamic.

For example:

If you have working parents and your kids are in after-school care.

If the parents are divorced and the kids want to keep in touch with both parents at all times.

If you have close relatives or friends, and either you move away or they do and the kids want to keep in touch with their best friends or cousins.

Basically, I don't vote for a specific age. Do I think a five-year-old should have a phone? No. A seven-year-old even? No. But I also don't know how each family functions. I vote for what is best for each individual family dynamic.

With all that said, I'm 1,000 percent gonna be the mom that goes through my kids' phones, iPads, and computers anytime I see fit. As long as I pay for your electronics, I have an all-access pass to them. The internet can be a crazy, toxic place full of creeps and trolls and bullies. And this mom is going to stick to her kids' devices like white on rice when the time comes to check their phones, iPads, or whatever hot new gadget exists. I believe in respecting teens' privacy...when they are going to the bathroom, grooming, or changing clothes. That's it. That's the only privacy my teens will get.[†]

[†]*Disclaimer: Neither Tommy nor I have raised a preteen and/or teenager, so our thoughts are purely speculation-based. There is a fairly good chance we will eat crow after raising our own teenagers. Crow pie. Crow burgers. Crow upon crow. Stay tuned.*

It's interesting, as I was thinking through all the ins and outs on this topic, there's one item that I'm actually leaning toward. I figured that once my kids launched after high school and college, I would insist that they foot the bill for their cell coverage. But now I'm starting to think I'd want to keep them on the family plan for a while, reason being, family plans are a less expensive and far more economical way to handle cell bills! So, in a surprise move from Ye Ol' Frugal Tommy, I'm considering keeping them on the family cell plan as they start into their adult lives and careers. I don't want their bills going up. I've been saving money this whole time for the benefit of my kids, although I'm not sure they see it that way...yet.

Alright, ladies and gentlemen, it's time for you to choose whose side you are on!

From the mom corner...Kids are getting cell phones and tablets at younger and younger ages, and sometimes for good reason. There shouldn't be some arbitrary age at which kids should or shouldn't have cell phones; it needs to be evaluated based on each family's lifestyle and needs.

From the dad corner...Kids don't need cell phones until at least high school, and even then, they don't need the latest and greatest smartphone. A phone should be for older kids, and should only be for keeping in touch with Mom and Dad, not a device that traps them in distraction and endless social media binges.

Whose side are you on...MOM or DAD?

Should Pets Be Allowed on the Furniture?

I am a dog lover.

I was raised by dog lovers.

I grew up in a house with eleven older siblings who were all dog lovers.

Having twelve kids wasn't enough chaos for my parents; they always had two or three dogs in the house throughout our childhood. And these weren't little dogs by any account. These were Saint Bernards, Great Danes, German shepherds, coonhounds, and always always always a Labrador retriever. You want to know the greatest dog breed for families with kids? Get yourself a Lab.

My lady speaks the truth. When we go to visit her family in Chicago, yes, everybody is excited about new babies. Baby puppies, that is. For real, they are very excited about new human babies, but they are almost as excited about puppies as well. There are over seventy grandkids and great-grandkids, but there might be even more puppies. The amount of drool, house-training, odd smells, and overall uncleanliness because of the family's dogs is astounding.

Unlike Tommy, I believe I have dog in my DNA. Hear me out.

You see, after birth, I was licked clean by our family's Saint Bernard. My mom delivered me at home with a midwife and home-birth doctor while my dad and siblings watched in awe, most hoping for a baby boy! The family had six girls and five boys…if I were a boy it would have been the Brady Bunch times two!!

Alas, I was a girl.

After a rock star birth of her twelfth child weighing an even nine pounds on a fish scale, it was time for a champagne toast honoring my mom. Listen, we're Irish, so as soon as the babe comes out, the mom celebrates with alcohol. So they laid me at the end of the bed, and our family's Saint Bernard, Gretchen, walked up and began licking me clean. As my dad yelled to stop her, it was the home-birth doctor that actually stopped him and said, "No, let her lick her, these two are going to have to live together in this house."

I hope this followed with a real bath, because, well, you were a human child after all.

For the first three years of my life, everywhere I went, Gretchen went. Everything I ate, Gretchen ate…and everything Gretchen ate, I ate too! I can thank my furry mom, Gretchen, for my superhuman immunity.

With that history, of course I treat my dogs like my babies.

While our Saint Bernard, Duke, provides the entertainment for our family, our black Lab, Duchess, provides security, devotion, and loyalty. And, like my children, I love my furry babies with all my heart; they both play an important and meaningful role in our family dynamic.

DOG MOM FOR LIFE!

Now that I'm a mom, I completely understand WHY my parents insisted on multiple dogs in a house full of kids. It's because kids can be jerks. Kids can demand and throw tantrums and whine and yell and complain…no matter what age! And without fail, Mom and Dad always get the brunt of the worst behavior. And that's okay, it means my kids feel safe to fall apart and know they are still unconditionally loved. And they most definitely are! But parenting is exhausting, you have no idea what will trigger your kid to implode…now multiply that by twelve kids.

Our family dogs were the first line of defense, frontline infantry. When one of us walked through that door after school, there they were, our loyal and lovable pups, ready to adore us for just being us, no judgment, no expectations! Speech issues, being dumped by a boyfriend, rejected by mean girls, failed a test…it did not matter. You were home and you immediately felt loved.

Let's get to the subject matter at hand. A big part of me feeling loved is having a clean couch to sit on and a nonsmelly bed to sleep in. A clean, comfy couch and a fresh bed help me think that I've made it in life. And Lucy has some boundary issues when it comes to where our dogs should sleep and nap and generally lounge.

Growing up, dogs also acted as Switzerland when you were in an all-out war with your siblings…and we used to have a lot of them. Our dogs ensured that common space, a safe zone between us kids when we were ready to throw down.

What does this have to do with dogs on furniture? Well, I

strongly believe that the dogs in my life played a major role. Each was considered a very important member of the family. Besides my parents, they were the MVPs of the house. They went where their paws took them, which included being on the bed, on the couch, under the dining room table, in the pool, on our family trips. Everywhere.

Sure! Take the dogs everywhere...except for the couch and bed, which just so happens to be what this chapter is about. It's not about MVPs, sibling wars, and the size of your family, so...

I have vivid memories of cuddling on the couch in the TV room with my black Lab as she lay over my legs and feet, acting as a weighted, heated blanket...which came in handy when your father believed fifty-five degrees was a suitable temperature during the brutal Chicago winters.

- You do realize what happens on the underbelly of dogs, right? Gross!
- Your dad worked two full-time jobs for decades because he had to feed twelve kids and countless dogs! Lay off about the thermostat...(And read more about our argument on it in chapter 15, "Who Should Control the Thermostat?")

Moral of the story. Dogs are the friggin' BEST!

I am married to a man who was not raised as a dog lover. But he has come a long way in the years since we met. We started with adopting a wheaten terrier when we were newlyweds without kids.

Mr. Bojangles was an eight-year-old senior pup whose previous male owner passed away. He immediately took to Tommy. He was a nice transitional dog who lived out his final years with us.

Um...you're telling me this was part of a three-step program I was in, unbeknownst to me?

Next came our black Lab. Once I had a family of my own, naturally, I needed a black Lab to complete the equation. I had a two-year-old toddler (though she was a runner more than a toddler) and a four-month-old, so just like my mom, I added chaos on top of chaos. Our family adopted a four-month-old pup, and we named her Duchess. Now if you ask my children, I have no shame in admitting that Duchess is "my best-behaved child" and the three other kids are tied at "second best behaved." And they have no issue with this and celebrate Duchess's elevated position because THANKFULLY all of my kids took after Mommy in being massive dog lovers.

Yes, yes they are. And unfortunately, they try to trick me into scenarios in which I can get slobbered on, and my clothing covered in dog hair. It's all fun and games until somebody shows up to work in black clothes covered by Saint Bernard hair. That's right, Lucy's told you about our original wheaten terrier and our Labrador, but there's also a huge Saint Bernard in this dog tale. (See what I did there?)

As I said, building our dog family has been a process. Once I had Tommy mostly locked in at liking dogs, it was time for the big ask, the one for which I needed reinforcements from each of my kids. And that big ask was,

"Can we get a Saint Bernard?"

The record should state that there was never "a big ask." Rather, it was subtly assumed by all three kids and their mom that we were getting a Saint Bernard. My opinion was never part of the equation.

As luck would have it, my neighbor's dog was having a litter of Saint Bernard puppies, which was rare in SoCal. It was my only chance! And thanks to a VERY persuasive firstborn (Babs ran starter on this one, sweetly begging and pleading for a puppy), Tommy said yes! Now our family is complete with Duke and Duchess.

But this agreement was reached under one, and only one, condition with Tommy. He stipulated that no dogs be allowed on our bed or on the furniture. Now to be fair, Saint Bernards are known to produce the most slobber out of all dog breeds, and being one of the biggest dog breeds of all time also leads to big shedding.

You're telling me. Sheesh. As I type this, there is Saint Bernard hair floating around me. I've had to change two sweatshirts already this morning, because the first ones were overwhelmed by white dog hair.

But I have faith that my days of cuddling my puppies on the couch are in the not-so-distant future. Not to brag, but I transformed a non–dog lover into a dog lover, and not just any dog lover…a Saint Bernard–loving, drool-attracting owner!

No, no, and no! I mean, yes, I love our dogs, but no, you have reached the extent of your powers, my bride. It honestly makes no sense to me, the lady that stresses over a clean house wants dogs on the couches and bed?

An ideal day for our pups includes eating out of a garbage can, drinking out of a toilet, and wrestling in mud.

And man, their shedding, drool, and smell is everywhere. And we want to put that on our couch?

I was germophobic before we voluntarily had kids and involuntarily got a few dogs, and now all I'm hoping for is a clean couch to sit on and a clean bed to sleep in. Those are the only things left in this house that aren't stinky!

Lucy and the kids would truly welcome the dogs on every piece of furniture and bed in the house, and I'm convinced that part of the reason they want this is because they know how much it bugs me.

Our oldest daughter asked me the other day if we can have six dogs. We currently have two, so that would mean adding four more. Can you imagine the mess and smell?

I've learned to love my dogs, but I just want one tiny part of my house clean...where I sit and sleep. Keep the beds and couches clean and dog-free, please!

Alright, ladies and gentlemen, it's time for you to choose whose side you are on!

From the mom corner…Dogs are part of the family and should have the same rights as any family member, which includes comfy places to nap and cuddle. My favorite places to nap and cuddle are the couch and my bed, so Duke and Duchess have every right to join me there. Family is family, canine or human.

From the dad corner…I've given in. As somebody who was not born a dog person, I've become one for my family. The dogs have taken over our lives, but I just need two sacred spots free of dog hair and drool: my couches and our bed. Give them everything else! Vote no to pets spending time on furniture and beds.

Whose side are you on…MOM or DAD?

To Have or Not to Have Decorative Pillows?

There are few things that bother me more in life than seeing my wife come home with decorative pillows.

There are few things I love more in life than a home adorned with decorative pillows.

These things can go for twenty to fifty dollars per pillow, and I find them absolutely useless. We have decorative pillows in our bedroom. We have decorative pillows in the living room. We even have some decorative pillows on our back patio. We have year-round decorative pillows, and we have holiday season decorative pillows. Some of our evergreen pillows have floral patterns. Some have no pattern except for ugly. Ugh.

Babe, they are pillow shams. The holiday pillows you speak of are actually our regular pillows covered by shams. Breathe!

Shams? It sounds like a sham. I've never heard of such a thing. If that is the truth, that will help me breathe a little better. But there is still something really bugging me, and that's the shape of decorative pillows. When you get a normal pillow for a bed, you have a general idea of how it will be shaped. With decorative pillows, some might be square. Some might be circular. Some might be shaped like a hot dog bun. We have a couple that are about one foot by four feet and extremely puffy. Those cylinder-shaped decorative pillows might be my least favorite thing in the world.

Noted. Now I know what to get you for your birthday.

The hardest thing for me to swallow about this extensive decorative pillow collection is that these pillows are absolutely useless.

I've never seen anybody use a decorative pillow. Decorative pillows serve no purpose, and yet *they* must be served. They have to be moved out of the way to make room on the couch for people to sit, and they always end up on the floor. And then they have to be returned to the couch once the human sitters leave. Nobody rests their back or head on a decorative pillow.

When you go to sleep at night, guess what you have to do with all the decorative pillows piled on your bed? Yep, that's right. They have to be pushed to the floor, just like their couch cousins. Frankly, I'd just like to burn them.

Clearly, I've struck a sore spot. Can I get you a pillow for that raw nerve?

There has been only one time in my life that I have used decorative pillows, and that time is right now as I write this. I'm propped up in bed, laptop open, and I looked at the pillows on the floor as I was typing these last few words. I moved them up from the floor back onto the bed so I can use them as a barrier. Our baby girl is sleeping in bed next to me (Lucy is out of town), and I've stacked two decorative pillows on top of each other to my left, to stop the light on my laptop from disturbing her.

So, yes. In my over forty years of life, the only use I've found for a decorative pillow is as a light barrier.

This is all coming from a guy who had five couches in his apartment when we met. Clearly, he does not appreciate the aesthetic of a nicely decorated home. And if you are like me and can't quite afford expensive furniture and an interior designer, decorative pillows are a fantastic alternative! They immediately change the dynamic of a room, be it bedroom, living room, or patio. A lot of our home furniture is a compilation of what the previous owner left when they moved and some hand-me-downs from Tommy's parents. This results in a lot of mismatched furniture. Decorative pillows can tie them all together. I like to believe you can keep a beautiful home no matter your economic status.

Do you have Ikea pockets with Pottery Barn taste? Decorative pillows for the win!

Well, dang....Because these decorative pillows are so oddly shaped, they just rolled off each other and woke up my sleeping daughter. Normal pillows never start moving on their own. Okay, my brief appreciation is over. I hate decorative pillows!

Alright, ladies and gentlemen, it's time for you to choose whose side you are on!

From the mom corner...Decorative pillows are an inexpensive solution to beautifying any home or patio. You don't need to be a millionaire to have a stylish home. All you need are decorative pillows.

From the dad corner...Decorative pillows are nonfunctional, pricey, usually unattractive, and overall useless. Do what's best for the world and say goodbye to these space wasters!

Whose side are you on...MOM or DAD?

Top Sheets: To Use or Not to Use?

When you're feeling hot or stressed, they calm you down. When you're cold and in the middle of winter depression, they keep you warm. They care for you unconditionally.

Yes, a top sheet is always there for you. My top sheet has been with me every day of my life.

And here I thought he was describing his wife…nope, just a top sheet.

Long, long before I met Lucy, I was in love with my top sheet. I remember many warm summer nights as a child lying in bed and listening to baseball on AM radio. With no air-conditioning in the home, I had a fan on, and somehow my beloved top sheet helped to keep me cool. It was magical.

On cold winter nights as a child, I had a few blankets on top of my top sheet, but my friend was still there. It was the guiding fabric of my bedtime routine, the one constant 365 nights a year. Sure, you're cold for a minute with a top sheet leading the way in the winter, but as soon as you warm up under those covers, the top sheet then blends into the warm blanket, giving you a comfortable and peaceful night of rest.

I will undoubtedly continue to use top sheets for the rest of my life. However, I've married somebody who has zero respect for the top sheet that I love so much.

I didn't realize I was required to respect a bedsheet. Duly noted.

That's right, my wife does not care for the top sheet. Let me rephrase. It's not that she doesn't care for the top sheet. She doesn't really think about it. She barely acknowledges it to be honest. She doesn't even care that it's there. To her, it seems to be an annoyance. She doesn't understand that the top sheet is a necessary part of my lifelong bedtime routine. In some ways, that's what hurts the most, her apathy, her indifference, for this important piece of bedtime tradition.

Listen to this. Lucy would rather have a heavy comforter on her in the summer while blasting the AC than trust in the magic of the top sheet.

Truth. I like the weight of a blanket, no matter what season or temperature. I can sleep anywhere, as long as I have a pillow, my body pillow, and some sort of blanket. These weighted blankets are all the rage now because studies have proven the heaviness of the blanket provides comfort and security. As far as I know, there has been no such study done on top sheets.

Wow, fighting words there with no consideration for the feelings of top sheets worldwide, and those of us that love them. I'll do a study on top sheets right now. THEY ARE FREAKIN' AWESOME!

While I'm holding on to my top sheet for my dear life, Lucy has no issue with kicking the top sheet to the foot of the bed, and to not even pull it up when making the bed! Sheesh!

Ladies and gentlemen, clearly I've hit a nerve with Tommy.

The only time I can accept not having a top sheet is when you are at one of those fancy hotels where they have those amazing duvets that seem to have an intuitive air conditioner and heating unit built into them. You know what I mean? Those giant, high-thread-count duvets that somehow keep you comfortable regardless of the temperature. Oh, shoot, I apologize...I can't stand the words "thread count" and "duvet." I wish I hadn't just said them.

Well, at hotels, Tommy cranks the AC to the lowest of low temps...unlike home. (See also our chapter 15, titled "Who Should Control the Thermostat?")

Let's talk about room temperature for a minute. Actually, let's save that for the thermostat conversation. You know why? ROOM TEMPER- ATURE DOESN'T MATTER WITH A TOP SHEET! A top sheet keeps you comfortable regardless of the nighttime conditions you are in.

Just a few years ago I realized for the first time that there is a large population who does not use the top sheet (I know, I was shocked too), and for them, I have a few important questions:

1. Who do you think you are by turning down the top sheet?

We are not bedding snobs.

2. Have you ever experienced the thrill of the top sheet?

Not sure I want to know what type of "thrill" you experi-ence with your top sheet, Tommy…although now I'm a little bit concerned. Is this why you go to sleep each night so early? So you and "top sheet" can have some special time?

3. Are you a psycho?

No! I'm a descendant of Scotch Irish Vikings who slept where their boots landed. There was no top sheet needed, the stars above acted as a layer of comfort, reminding them that they survived another day. And if my ancestors didn't need top sheets, neither do I! (Spoken in a Scotch Irish accent.)

The fact that this is even a topic makes me laugh. To me, it's just another thing to wash, another step to making the bed, another item to fold, all of which I could use a lot less of in my life. And who knows, maybe the top sheet is simply a conspiracy on the part of Big Bedding to make us all think more sheets are a necessary part of beds. I won't fall for that kind of market manipulation.

The only thing top sheets are good for is toga parties, and I am fully supportive of top sheet culture in that situation. That is the only time I need a top sheet on my body.

Alright, ladies and gentlemen, it's time for you to choose whose side you are on!

From the mom corner…Take the minimalist message to your bedding. Make your bed more efficient and skip the extra step. Top sheets don't add anything to the sleep experience.

From the dad corner…This is the biggest no-brainer in the history of bedding. Top sheets have the ability to cool, warm, protect, and love you. Top sheets for life!

Whose side are you on…MOM or DAD?

ROUND
38

How Often Should You Wash Your Comforter?

I mean, this is DIRECTLY related to the top sheet debate. (See chapter 37, "Top Sheets: To Use or Not to Use?") And it's also DIRECTLY related to whether dogs should be sleeping on the bed. (See chapter 35, "Should Pets Be Allowed on the Furniture?") This topic is the nexus, one of the cornerstones of both my linen and my pet philosophies.

If you respect the top sheet and don't allow pets on the bed, your comforter is going to be just fine. It will last for a long time without needing to be washed. Comforters take multiple spin cycles to wash and dry, and for some reason, one of my major goals in life is to wash our comforter as little as possible.

A comforter is like a wig. It looks nice on the outside, but it is there for a reason, to cover something up. In the case of a bed, a comforter is covering up the sheets and blankets below it. Yes, it's a nice extra layer of warmth, but its main job is just to look pretty.

Kinda like decorative pillows? Tommy's understanding of the use of our comforter is the same approach I have to my decorative pillows, purely ornamental instead of functional. And while I will defend my love for decorative pillows to the death, comforters are there to comfort, and have a functional use.

Top sheets and blankets are there to do the hard work. They lie beneath you and on top of you, creating the perfect warmth sandwich. They protect the mattress, quell the dust mites, and create layers for a hygienic experience while you sleep. The comforter is just a bonus. It's the cherry on top. It is there to finish off the bed.

Who are you kidding? Comforters are basically glorified blankets. Most people don't sleep with a top sheet, and then a blanket and then a comforter. It's redundant to not rely on a comforter instead of some complexity of sheets and blankets.

I sleep with a top sheet, a blanket, *and* a comforter in the winter, and it is glorious.

Back to the topic at hand, how often to wash a comforter. If you are allowing the heroic top sheet to do its job, there is literally no reason for the bottom side of a comforter to ever get dirty.

If you are respecting your partner's space, and not allowing hairy, smelly, and drooly pets on the bed, the top side of the comforter should stay reasonably clean for a really long time. If you can do your best to never eat or drink in your room (and certainly not allow your kids to eat in there), a comforter could go a year without needing to be washed.

So basically you're asking me to not allow all the things that bring me joy (dogs, kids, and food) in or around OUR bed. Got it.

It's rather simple. At least it was until DOWN comforters were introduced. Yeah, you know those bulky, puffy, and incredibly soft comforters that are impossible to wash. Once down comforters came along, people (including my wife) started treating them like blankets, sheets, and a comforter all in one! It's so amazing, it keeps you warm, it cools you off, and it's so darn cuddly!

But the problem is you can't easily wash these mothers. Well, you can, but then the down starts magically disappearing or starts congregating into odd lumps in the corners. Does it disintegrate in the washer? Maybe. Does the dryer turn the down feathers into some kind of gas? Maybe. Regardless of the science, when they come out of a wash/dry sequence, they are never quite the same, like your favorite movie star who got a bit too aggressive with the Botox and a round of fillers. You gotta know when to stop. When we had a down comforter, my wife continued to wash it until it was completely ruined.

And I know what you're thinking...you just need a duvet cover. Put the down comforter into a duvet, they tell you. Oh, how I can't stand duvet covers. Putting the down comforter into a duvet is like trying to put a dog into a bathtub. It is a three-person job. Trying to get the comforter evenly into all four corners of the duvet is my worst nightmare, requiring some kind of wizardry and pagan sacrifice. Not even Martha Stewart (and I know this to be fact because I took a moment to scan the World Wide Web) can do it easily. She has an instructional video online, and it takes over five minutes to complete this complex maneuver, with her haranguing one of her stage managers, who is trying to help. And the buttons on duvet covers...I can't stand you. Hold on, I need a minute...(She also makes the stage manager help put all these decorative pillows on the bed, criticizing his technique. I may or may not have developed hives watching this torture.)

While Tommy takes a minute, I want to share a story, more like an epiphany I had years ago in the aisles of Bed Bath & Beyond. First a little backstory. Ever since Tommy and I started dating, he was the guy that slept with a box of tissues next to his bed (not for that reason, get your mind out of the gutter) and would spend a good majority of the night sneezing and coughing. He reminded me of the guy that Meg Ryan was engaged to in *Sleepless in Seattle* before meeting Tom Hanks. His nightstand was adorned with nasal spray, Kleenex, water, Tylenol—basically a bedside pharmacy.

I loved my guy, so I accepted him for what he was, apparently a sneezy sleeper. I figured the bedside pharmacy would become part of my decor landscape, too, when we got married, and was already coming up with strategies to make his collection look a little more refined, maybe contained in a chic basket or something like that. So here we were, months away from the big day, roaming the aisles of Bed Bath & Beyond. Tommy and I were selecting items for our wedding registry and had entered the bedding section. We started testing different pillows that we liked. Now, in the late 1990s and early 2000s, down pillows and comforters were ALL the rage. You knew you had reached a certain status if you had down bedding and linens with a certain thread count.

As we were testing those pillows, Tommy burst into a sneezing fit, and tissues from all eighty pockets in his cargo shorts were being excavated from the depths and used. It was obnoxious, the constant sneezing and nostril blowing, so we moved on to the bath section. I immediately noticed I got my fiancé back. Sneezing, coughing, and a nasally voice had all disappeared in a matter of moments.

Epiphany.

Me: Tommy, are you allergic to down?

Tommy: What? No. I mean, I don't think so…

Me: Come here!

I dragged him back to the bedding section, where he erupted into sneezing and sniffling all over again.

Me: OMG, you are allergic to down. ALL of your bedding is made of down!

This poor kid has literally had down pillows and blankets since college. It seems so obvious now looking back, but no one had ever made the connection. So, in addition to stealing his heart, I had cured and cleared Tommy's nasal passages. Lucy for the win! (And the crowd goes wild.)

Lucy did indeed change my life with that realization. We eliminated down from the house and got those down alternative comforters as a replacement. The allergy issue was eliminated but, alas, the laundering of those new comforters presented the same challenges as my old down comforter nemesis, the endless wash-and-dry cycles, the weirdly shaped lumps that result after washing a bulky comforter. Today, we have gone retro and taken it way back, all the way to a standard, old-school quilt. And when we have to wash it, it is much easier to deal with, but still requires two to three cycles in the dryer to get the thing dry.

To recap, let's get back to basics. If you don't allow a dog in your bed, and you use top sheets as they were meant to be used, you should be able to get away with washing a comforter only a couple of times each year.

But it's in the actual name! Comforters are like clothes, socks, robes, and jackets…they are all made to provide warmth and comfort to humans. You know what else provides comfort to humans? Dogs. Who needs a top sheet *and* comforter when you can have a 140-pound Saint Bernard puppy as your blanket!?!

We regularly wash our clothes, socks, and robes, so why wouldn't we use this "glorified blanket" the same way?! You should definitely be washing your comforter every few weeks at the very least!

Alright, ladies and gentlemen, it's time for you to choose whose side you are on!

From the mom corner…Live your best life, use your comforter just as you would any other piece of adored clothing or blanket, and launder it at will.

From the dad corner…Respect the comforter. Consider it a semipermanent form of upholstery. Protect it from unnecessary wear and tear by adding a top sheet to your bedding repertoire and by keeping muddy dogs and greasy popcorn off its snowy surface.

Whose side are you on…MOM or DAD?

ROUND
39

Is It Okay to Fake Symptoms to Get Out of Sex?

If you are female and have never faked a symptom to get out of sex with your partner, then congratulations on not being human.

And before I get into this, let me preface it by saying I enjoy sex with my man. I really do. But sometimes I fall into a rut, both physically and mentally, and sex is just another task on my already never-ending to-do list. I know that sounds bad but it's my truth. Between my kids, my dogs, my job, and yes, even my husband, I often feel totally defeated and depleted by the end of the day.

> Hi there! It's me, your super-handsome husband over here. Want to get all of that off your mind and have sex?

I will admit that even when I'm not completely feeling up for sex, I have never regretted it once it was done. I then would often realize that I needed that contact, that connection a lot more than I thought. The benefits of doing the deed far exceed not doing it.

So why in the world would I not want to do it, you might ask? Well, I'm about to get 100 percent real, all of y'all. I'm going to break down the excuses we use versus the real reasons we are too embarrassed to admit in the moment.

Here's what we say followed by what we really mean:

"I have a headache."

Code for: I'm exhausted because our kids kicked my butt today and I keep replaying the epic meltdown our kid had at the park and beating myself up for not handling it better.

Babe, I'm sorry that you're stressed. Let's hug it out, then make out?

"I feel like I might have food poisoning."

Code for: I have horrible gas from that egg salad sandwich I ate earlier, and I fear you will never find me attractive again if one were to rip during the deed.

Okay, yeah, just stick to the food poisoning.

"I pulled a muscle rearranging the furniture."

Code for: I feel about as sexy as a beached whale after trying on bathing suits at the mall, and the thought of getting naked right now makes me cringe. Also, I probably should not have chosen pasta for lunch moments before hitting the beach shop.

Pulling a muscle rearranging furniture is kind of sexy, so I'm not sure if this code example really works...

"I just watched this super-disturbing docuseries on Netflix."

Code for: My mind is not in a good place but I don't want you to think I'm a crazy person. Also, probably not a good idea to watch the news, scroll through Twitter, or binge that murder-suicide docuseries, if there is any chance sex could be in the cards.

I will never again recommend we watch *Beware the Slenderman*. That was a self-inflicted wound, brought on by me.

"I just got a spray tan and cannot shower for the rest of the day."

Code for: I'm just too tired to shower and put forth the effort to go through the whole post-shower routine.

Bad excuse! If you have time for a spray tan, you have time for me!

And why do we fake symptoms and not use the root causes? Because a lot of times the real reasons might be interpreted by our partner as a rejection. And no one likes to feel rejected. But if we say something that is personal to us, it decreases the chances of our partner feeling hurt or offended. Plus, I don't want my exhaustion from that particular day to affect the chances of future sexy sessions.

Admittedly, I'm usually the one to turn down sex…but there has been a time or two in the past decade where Tommy was the one who turned down the opportunity. And I learned that it's really hard not to take it personally, even when your partner's reasons are completely valid.

So, I'm all for a little white lie, a fake excuse, if it means Tommy is less likely to take it personally and his ego (and libido) will still come on to me in the future.

(*Waits five minutes.*)

Want to go have sex?

Alright, ladies and gentlemen, it's time for you to choose whose side you are on!

From the mom corner...Sometimes you feel like it, sometimes you don't. A well-played excuse is a good way to preserve your partner's dignity and confidence.

From the dad corner...We understand that it won't always work out how we envision, but if many other things are prioritized high in life, we wish that sex could be as well.

Whose side are you on...MOM or DAD?

ROUND
40

Toilet Paper:
Over or Under?

I have no idea why I love UNDER so much, but I do. I always have, and I always will. I know I'm in the minority here, but I have to stand firm to my long-held beliefs.

He might not know, but I know exactly why Tommy loves under so much. Never in our years of dating and being married did he ever mind my OVER placement of the toilet paper roll. It was a nonissue. But then one day he overheard a heated conversation I was engaged in with some friends, where I made the mistake of sharing my absolute loathing for when someone places a toilet paper roll UNDER instead of OVER.

Guess what happened next? Every time I went to use the bathroom, the toilet paper roll would now suddenly be UNDER.

Son of a....!

You guys, it's in his freaking name…if he knows he can get a rise out of me, Tommy Riles riles me up and loves every minute of it!

That's nice that Lucy thinks she's the reason I opt for UNDER. She's certainly the reason behind my opinion on many topics, but not this one...I've been on TEAM UNDER for as long as I can remember.

UNDER isn't just a simple decision...it is a much smarter way of life! I have great comfort knowing I have to simply reach UNDER the roll, and pull the TP out easily.

I've had way too many instances where when I'm working with an OVER roll I have to tug too firmly, and just one sheet rips off. I try again, and then a second sheet rips off. Then a third. And then what do I do? Place all three small pieces of toilet paper together and use them? Or do I keep trying and wasting more soft paper?

I googled this topic recently to figure out why I love UNDER so much, and I got my answer: cats! Stay with me...when you have a cat, they are likely to go into the bathroom and start unrolling toilet paper easily with their paws if it is OVER. They'll then keep unraveling the roll until it is complete. However, if the roll is UNDER, they won't be able to unravel it at all.

Guess how many cats Tommy has owned or cared for in his place of residence in the forty plus years of his life? ZERO.

Therefore, you cannot use cats as a reason to rebel against the proper roll standards.

Well, I did house-sit for our neighbors' cats a few times in the early 1990s, and if I recall correctly, I may have seen a toilet paper mess in their bathroom in May of '92. They must have left for vacation lazily leaving the toilet paper rolls in the OVER position.

Here's my final hypothesis on this topic: If you are using UNDER, you are helping to save planet Earth. If you are using OVER, you are wasting TP, and ruining our environment.

By the way, if you are a big fan of OVER and you see me on the street, no need to tell me that the patent for a toilet paper roll shows that OVER is the correct way. I get it, many people have brought that up to me. My counterargument would be to look at Edison's patent on the light bulb from 1880. Have light bulbs changed in every which way since then? Yes! Are there greener-style light bulbs than the ones from 1880? You better believe it. Innovation is necessary for us all to grow. UNDER for life!

This isn't even worth my time to rebut; obviously the only way to properly install a roll of toilet paper is OVER.

But let's talk about the real crime committed in this debate…the culprits who use those last sheets of toilet paper without replacing the roll (*points interrogation light at my son*). Now, this inevitably leads to the next victim (aka Mom or Dad) left out to dry, or in the very worst-case scenario, left in a super-crappy situation. Literally.

Alright, ladies and gentlemen, it's time for you to choose whose side you are on!

From the mom corner…OVER. It's the only way to go.

From the dad corner…UNDER isn't just a decision, it's a movement. Do you want to be a greener, smarter, and better person? TEAM UNDER is where you want to be.

Whose side are you on…MOM or DAD?

How to Properly Use Toothpaste Tubes

May I present to the jury, our readers, exhibit A.

The way my husband and children use toothpaste tubes is absolutely barbaric. I imagine this is what toothpaste tubes would look like if they were around during the Stone Age.

I just can't.

Just as there is only one way to install a toilet paper roll, there is only one way to use a toothpaste tube. You squeeze from the very bottom as needed until your toothpaste tube looks as though a steamroller plowed over it. I take great personal pride in my ability to render a toothpaste tube into a configuration that is reminiscent of the way pasta dough looks after being run through a pasta maker: flat, serene, no lumps, no wrinkles.

And this should go without saying for any civilized human being; you neatly screw the toothpaste cap back onto the toothpaste tube. If you carelessly skip the toothpaste cap step, like my husband the toothpaste barbarian does, you risk toothpaste remnants hardening around the only point of exit for the toothpaste. Failure to successfully apply the cap begins a buildup process of hardened toothpaste that multiplies and multiplies and multiplies with each use. Ultimately this buildup will completely block the opening of the tube, thus making the remaining toothpaste inaccessible and thus wasted. (I never realized how often one uses the word "thus" in the evidentiary process of exhibiting toothpaste tube proof. I feel quite fancy.)

For the guy who is super frugal, his toothpaste tube game is both wasteful and costly. Tommy, you are clearly throwing away hard-earned cash. And that, my darling, is all on you.

And while we are on the topic of toothpaste caps, I would like to share with the jury one of my BIGGEST pet peeves about my dearly beloved during the toddler years of our children's lives.

In addition to not easily placing the cap back on the toothpaste tube, Tommy will proceed to lose the cap or drop it on the floor. Apparently, the effort one would exert to bend over and pick up such an item is just too much for Tommy to commit to.

The issue was that when our kids were toddlers, those adorable mini versions of yourself that crawl and climb and toddle their way into everything, they would put anything they could find into their mouths. I lived in constant fear that one of them would find the toothpaste cap Tommy couldn't be bothered to locate, and would immediately place that errant cap in his or her mouth. I think it is safe to say, although I know there are exceptions, that most moms tend to worry a tad more than dads. The sheer terror moms play out in their minds of a baby choking on something is all-consuming during the toddler stage.

So when I would find a toothpaste cap, shaped in a way that could so easily lodge into a baby's throat, I would legit lose sleep over it, finding myself scoping the bathroom floors for any sign of toothpaste caps.

JUST PUT THE CAP ON THE FREAKING TOOTHPASTE!

The good news...we safely survived the toddler years without a toothpaste cap incident, no thanks to Tommy!

The bad news...he has passed down his grossly negligent toothpaste etiquette to our children.

I squeeze the toothpaste from the middle. I know that is the unpopular choice in our culture today. But I make up for it by pushing all of the toothpaste to the top once the tube is almost empty. I have a superpower that way. Just when everybody else has lost hope that there is any toothpaste left, I will work hard to squeeze out more. I make miracles happen, really. My wife and kids should be thankful for my skills.

You might be wondering why I don't just squeeze from the bottom of the tube the entire time to avoid the extra work at the end of the tube's life cycle. Look, I believe there is a power in delayed gratification. I get quite a bit of satisfaction out of being able to make more toothpaste appear once others have given up hope. It's a spiritual discipline of mine.

Even though my toothpaste game might not be up to regulation, I can assure you that there is no toothpaste wasted on my watch; the toothpaste continues to be used regardless of how tough it is to get out of the tube. I accept that the midtube-squeeze condition of our toothpaste tubes is my doing, but that's just about style points, not about actual toothpaste waste.

For me, the biggest concern about brushing teeth in the household is how large a collection of toothbrushes we have for the kids. Lucy is always buying some new version of a pediatric toothbrush, units that light up, play music, spin, and dance. It's a challenge to keep up with the status of this extensive dental stock. And it doesn't reduce the amount of work it takes to get my progeny to practice reasonable dental hygiene.

Lucy will admit this: I'm much more involved in the kids' toothbrushing routine than she is, and my kids still fight off brushing their teeth with every opportunity they have. For children, brushing is not a fun time. And all the bells and whistles of the toothbrush collection aren't helping. And then there are the toothpaste options, a selection almost as extensive as the types of toothbrushes they have at their disposal. All three kids each have their own type of toothpaste, some of it in tube form, some in stand-up pump form, along with their action figure/Disney Princess/electric/singing/whirling toothbrush options. It all leads to more fights about who is using which toothbrush each day, arguing about whether one of the other kids is using "their" toothpaste, and endless debates on varying ownership and usage. So yeah, good times.

What about a simple toothbrush and just one tube of toothpaste for all three kids? All these options in life are making them too picky.

I'll tell you what, Lucy, here's a compromise. I'll start squeezing from the bottom of our toothpaste tube if you let me control the kids' toothbrush purchases from here on out. No need for all of this fancy stuff, it's not working!

I'm tempted. But I'll also need some ironclad agreements about toothpaste tube caps as well. Have your people get in touch with my people once you've considered my bathroom counteroffer...

Alright, ladies and gentlemen, it's time for you to choose whose side you are on!

From the mom corner...Squeeze those tubes from the bottom and replace those caps. Fight toothpaste waste with these simple practices; it might just help save the nice caps from melting. Any other practice makes you a barbarian.

From the dad corner...Accept the challenges in life, in whatever form they come. Attempt the remnant-of-the-tube challenge. As down and dirty as the tube gets, become more heroic by continuing to squeeze more toothpaste out of it. You've gotta test and push yourself every day! Perseverance is of the highest value here.

Whose side are you on...MOM or DAD?

A Few Final Thoughts

Thank you so much for reading our book and taking this journey with us.

As we said at the start, this book is meant to be fun...not an excuse to start bickering with your spouse. Relationships and raising a family are hard, so know that you are not alone in some of the day-to-day battles we covered in this book. And even though it might sound like we disagree on WAY TOO MUCH, this is all coming from a place of love for us. We recognize that we're both very different from each other, yet we work hard on making our relationship better every single year. Pardon our sappiness, but to balance out the battles we just went through, here are love letters we've written to each other:

Tommy,

Thank you for being the most incredible father to our kids. If not for you, our house would contain 99.98 percent less laughter in it. Your silly, fun-loving antics trigger belly laughs echoed throughout the house and in our hearts.

Thank you for working so hard for our family, often picking up extra gigs on weeknights and weekends so that we can live this perfectly imperfect life.

Thank you for being my rock, always strong and unwavering. To know me is to know I am full of emotions; some might even say I'm dramatic but I blame my fiery Irish temper. ☺ You are the optimist to my skeptic, the calm to my restlessness.

Thank you for supporting me and all my outrageous ideas. Even if you're thinking, "This girl has lost her mind," you just nod along and let me go for it, win or lose.

These past two hundred pages or so, we vehemently disagreed on most topics...but there's no other man I'd rather bicker with than you.

And here is where I go deep and metaphorical.

Life has taken our marriage in many directions; some smooth sailing, some weathering heart-wrenching storms...but we have faced each turn of the tide anchored in faith, hope, and love.

I love you more.

Lucy

Dearest Bride,

You are everything to me. And you have been ever since I saw you on the softball field. You were the only girl playing wearing a cowgirl hat and formfitting jean shorts, and I couldn't take my eyes off you. And I still can't.

The kids and I are so lucky to have such a passionate, kind, loving, and generous person in our lives. Your heart is beautiful on the inside, and your body is beautiful on the outside. Yeah, I said it.

I often can't comprehend the way you think about things (as we uncovered in the past two hundred pages), but I do my best to accept that we are just two different people who handle things very differently. And I love the way that you navigate life.

I think we have a wonderful (but certainly not perfect) marriage, and I look forward to spending the rest of my life with you.

I believe in you. I believe in us. I believe in our kids. Let's do this.

Still do? Me too.

Tommy

If you've enjoyed this book, be sure to check out the online parenting communities we have built called Life of Dad and Life of Mom! Just search @lifeofdad and @lifeofmom on Facebook or Instagram. We would love it if you shared with us some of your not-so-serious stuff you fight about with your significant other.

For more on us, follow @tommyriles and @lucyriles on Facebook and Instagram and give a listen to our podcast, *Mom vs. Dad*, for additional topics and a chance to be featured on our show. You call in and we battle the hot topics at hand.

Thanks again for reading our book, *Mom vs. Dad: Whose Side Are You On?* We really appreciate the support and hope you enjoyed the read!

We'll leave you with some words from Mother Teresa:

> *If you want to change the world,*
> *go home and love your family.*

Acknowledgments

To our parents; Barbara and Jim Bansley and Andrea and Tom Riles, for being the greatest role models of what it means to be a mom and dad, husband and wife to one another. For always showing us unconditional love that was deeply rooted in our faith in God. And for always supporting our dreams and providing wings to help us soar. We are forever grateful for the life and love you have given us.

To our Life of Mom and Life of Dad communities, thank you for joining us on this ride called parenthood. Your insight and support mean everything to us.

To Tommy's boss for almost two decades, Ellen DeGeneres, thank you for being there for our family during the highs and lows. And for teaching us how to bring kindness and positivity into the world every day. We love you.

We wish to express our sincerest gratitude to the amazing people that helped make this possible. More specifically, our literary agent, Priya Doraswamy, and editors; Karen Longino, Julie Lyles Carr, and the entire team at Hachette Book Group and Worthy Publishing. Thank you for taking a chance and believing in us.

With love and gratitude,
Lucy and Tom Riles

About the Authors

Lucy Riles is a mom to four children, two dogs, and a wife to one husband. In addition to her role as "human creator," Lucy is a writer, creator, storyteller, and founder of Life of Mom, a flourishing online community for moms. Lucy and her dog, Duchess, also competed on season one of Amazon's hit series *The Pack.*

Lucy grew up as the youngest of twelve kids on the South Side of Chicago. She was raised by two amazing parents, Barbara and Jim Bansley, who taught her early on the value of faith, love, and family. After graduating from Ball State University, Lucy moved to Los Angeles. There, she met her husband, Tommy Riles, founder of Life of Dad.

Tommy and Lucy's entrance into parenthood was anything but smooth. Their first child was born in 2010 with a serious heart condition requiring life-saving open-heart surgery at three days old. Because of this, and a devastating pregnancy loss, Lucy and Tommy are keenly aware that life and family are precious gifts not to be taken for granted.

Lucy and Tommy co-host an interactive comedy show as well as a comical podcast also called *Mom vs. Dad: Whose Side Are You On?*

Lucy's motto in life…ENJOY THE RIDE!

Tom Riles is the proud husband to Lucy Riles, father to four (plus two dogs), and the founder of the largest community of dads in the world, *Life of Dad*.

Additionally, Tom is one of the top audience warm-up comedians in Hollywood, having worked on over 200 television shows with crowds as large as 10,000 people. For over sixteen years, Riles has opened for *The Ellen DeGeneres Show* as well as Ellen's *Game of Games* and her *Relatable* tour.

Tom is also one of the co-creators of the hit international TV show *The Spyders*, as well as an investor/advisor to the lifestyle brand for dads *DADZ*.

Tom and Lucy co-host a comedy podcast called *Mom vs. Dad*, as well as a live interactive comedy show.

Born in New Jersey and raised along with his three sisters by super-parents, Tom Sr. and Andrea, Riles grew up in a loving household who always put family first. Riles graduated from the College of New Jersey and has worked in Los Angeles in the entertainment industry ever since.

Tommy's motto in life…ENJOY THE RIDE with Lucy Riles by my side.

For more from Lucy and Tom, check out
their parenting communities at:

lifeofmom.com

 @lifeofmom

 @lifeofmom

 @lifeofmomuncut

lifeofdad.com

 @lifeofdad

 @lifeofdad

 @lifeofdadshow

For more Mom vs. Dad, check out
Lucy and Tom's podcast at:

Mom vs. Dad:
Whose Side Are You On?
on Apple Podcasts

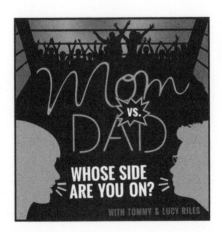